THE STORY OF
HISTORIC
FORT
STEUBEN

THE STORY OF
HISTORIC
FORT
STEUBEN

JOHN R. HOLMES, PhD

THE
History
PRESS

Published by The History Press
Charleston, SC 29403
www.historypress.net

All images courtesy Historic Fort Steuben unless otherwise noted.

First published 2010

ISBN 9781540234971

Library of Congress Cataloging-in-Publication Data

Holmes, John R. (John Robert), 1955-
The story of historic Fort Steuben / John R. Holmes.
p. cm.
Includes bibliographical references.
ISBN 9781540234971
1. Fort Steuben (Steubenville, Ohio) 2. Steubenville (Ohio)--History, Military. 3.
Fortification--Ohio--Steubenville--History. 4. Steubenville (Ohio)--Buildings, structures, etc.
I. Title.

F499.S8H66 2010
977.1'69--dc22
2010010833

CONTENTS

CONTENTS

INTRODUCTION

T his is the story of how Fort Steuben was built. Twice.
The first time, near the end of the eighteenth century, it took 150 soldiers thirty-three workdays to complete. The second time, near the end of the twentieth century, it took an army of volunteers, heavy equipment and a Tennessee construction company more than twenty years. Because Fort Steuben was built the first time, America was able to begin expanding beyond the borders of the original thirteen states. Because Fort Steuben was built a second time, the people of the upper Ohio Valley don't need to go to a book or a museum to see how their pioneer predecessors lived: they can see it right there on Third Street in Steubenville, between Adams and Market, looking virtually like the 1787 model—thanks to the meticulous records of a military bureaucracy and the pluck and plod of a couple of tenacious historian-entrepreneurs.

The story of that first raising of a fort in the wilderness is adventurous enough, but somehow the story of raising public interest (and raising public and private funds) can be nearly as exciting. Life at the fort in 1787 had its own dangers, of course, but an eighteenth-century soldier or surveyor didn't have to worry if there might be a scowling naysayer or a double-breasted bureaucrat behind every tree. Building a fort in the 1780s was not for the meek, and neither was rebuilding one in the 1980s. (And '90s. And beyond.)

The telling of that story, however, is relatively easy, because all of the real work had already been done decades before I got to the project by a few key members of the Old Fort Steuben Project, especially two who are no longer with us, Jack Boyde and Richard Q. King. Jack, the guiding force behind the archaeological dig that still continues every summer, passed away in October 2000. Dick, who with his wife Elizabeth headed the committee that started the whole project, died in February 2006. There is certainly a bit of Professor Boyde and a little of Mr. King in the heart of Fort Steuben, but there is also a great deal of both men in this book. I have been faithful to all of the written sources cited in my bibliography, but I could never begin to footnote each insight that these two educators brought to the reimagination of Fort Steuben. Anything in this account that rings true is probably due to something Jack or Dick told me. But more important, the affection for those massive blocks of hemlock that make up the fort, and for the memory of the men who built it in the first place—that love of reliving history that fires this narrative—a lot of that came from Dick and Jack, too.

So much of the story of Fort Steuben comes through these two men that, while I couldn't draw on their expertise during the writing of this book, perhaps it would be appropriate to let them speak here as best they can, from their words in the Steubenville *Herald Star* over the twenty years of the reconstruction. Dick King's reflections on Fort Steuben's role in renewing Steubenville are still inspiring a decade later:

> *This area was an empty lot with old railroad tracks and other items scattered all over it. Now we are building something positive that will be associated with downtown Steubenville as well as used as a building block to revitalize the entire city. Fort Steuben will provide something positive, illuminating, and beautiful for the people of Steubenville to see and take pride in. To change the community for the better, we have to offer something new. The image we leave is going to be here a lot of years. People are going to see something lovely and attractive for many years to come with Fort Steuben Park.*

Jack Boyde's observations about the dig at Fort Steuben are more succinct: "It's just a good place to teach archaeology. I think we'll be down there for another ten years." Twenty years after Jack said that, the dig is still going on in his name.

As for the current staff of Fort Steuben, so many of the members have influenced this account that I will certainly forget to mention some of them. But most directly bearing on the writing itself was a very helpful and motivating brainstorming session on November 16, 2009, with Judy Bratten and Jerry Barilla. Judy, the executive director of Fort Steuben, also helped me retrieve most of the images in this book from the fort archives and scanned them for me. So if a picture is worth a thousand words, then Judy contributed sixty thousand words to this book, which beats my contribution

Franciscan University of Steubenville archaeologist Professor Phil Fitzgibbons teaches children at the Fort Steuben Summer Educational Program, 2006.

by twenty thousand. Jerry, as the current president of the organization, has ably taken up the mantle left by Dick King as site manager and also took many of the photos included in this book. Andy Celestin, the fort's resident woodworker, by explaining the many artifacts he has re-created for Fort Steuben, has helped with my general understanding of life in 1787. Now if only I could find someone to explain life today.

Alan Hall, for many years the director of the Public Library of Steubenville and Jefferson County, should be thanked for the historical insights he has given me as an interpreter at Fort Steuben—should be, I say—but on the other hand, I figure that's his job as a librarian, so I will just thank him for the way too many laughs he has given me during long hours at the fort (and for the many lifts home he has given me).

Professor Phil Fitzgibbons was kind enough to look at an early draft of the prehistoric Indian material. I hope that the final draft here is accurate enough, or he may make me work on the dig next summer.

Mayor Dominick Mucci, like his predecessor, David Hindman, has always been a friend to Fort Steuben. That probably has no bearing on this book, but at a presentation last fall, Mayor Mucci kindly gave a plug for my first History Press book, *Remembering Steubenville: From Frontier Fort to Steel Valley*, and pretended to be miffed at not being mentioned in it. Well, he can't say that about this book. Thanks, Dom, for all you have done for the fort and for the city.

Finally, this book, or at least its author, owes a great deal to the people of Steubenville for asking the hundreds of questions over my twenty years as a spokesman for the fort and for their enthusiasm for the past. Since the first Fort Steuben Festival in 1991, I have been portraying Baron von Steuben, and my best audiences have been the very young and the very old. If the ones in between can imitate them in their zeal for our history, then Fort Steuben will thrive. If not, we will all be poorer.

OHIO BEFORE THE FORT

The Native Americans

One of the first questions visitors to Fort Steuben ask is: who were the Native Americans in the area when the fort was built? And the answer cannot be simple, because the upper Ohio Valley saw a history of migration, exile and forced removal of several tribes across the centuries. Who lived in the area before Fort Steuben was built? That depends on what century you're talking about. As early as 1000 BC, the Woodland people known as the Adena spread throughout southern Ohio and West Virginia, with significant settlements both upriver and downriver from the future home of Fort Steuben. Today's Appalachian residents think of this culture as the Mound Builders, since the most striking Adena remains are massive burial mounds throughout the region.

The Adena people were displaced by other cultures before they could hand down any oral traditions, so there is no native history of the Mound Builders that comes down to us. But study of the mounds reveals complex mortuary practices involving, apparently, the fullest artistic and religious expression of these nations. The cores of the mounds are mortuaries, which became crematoria; bodies were gathered, along with artifacts presumably useful in the afterlife. The whole structure was then burned and covered in earth—not just random dirt but carefully graded and collected earth. Once the mortuary was covered, another might be built on top of it, so that some mounds grew with each generation.

Adena artifacts are distinctive and clearly influence later Native American art. The use of copper from the Great Lakes and shells from

State of Ohio Historical Marker for Fort Steuben, with the northwest blockhouse in the background.

the Gulf Coast in this art indicates a sophisticated network of trade in this prehistoric period. One of the most remarkable types of work consists of small, flat stones, half an inch thick and measuring three by four to four by five inches. These stones bear relief carvings of animal shapes and geometric designs. Some bear traces of paint, leading to speculation that they may be stamps for placing the figures on clothing or skin—perhaps even as a template for tattooing.

The Adena culture thrived in the Ohio Valley for eight hundred years, until it was replaced by the Hopewell, migrating either from the east (western New York) or the west (Illinois) about 200 BC. The Hopewell designation is neither a nation, tribe nor culture but rather a general shared tradition among Native Americans who settled in, and adopted some traditions of, their mound-building predecessors. The Hopewell continued the Adena mound-building traditions but with some innovations. Some mounds became octagonal instead of circular, and late twentieth-century research suggests that they may have functioned as astronomical and lunar observatories. In Newark, Ohio, 130 miles southwest of Fort Steuben, the Fairground Circle is aligned to the point of local sunrise on May 4, the precise midpoint between the spring equinox and summer solstice. Thus, the eight points of the octagon designate not only the fourfold pattern of solstice and equinox but also the midpoints in between, or what astronomers call "cross-quarter" days.

At this point, the reader may be tempted to think that we started our history of Fort Steuben way too early. Surely nothing could be further from the story of an eighteenth-century military installation than speculation on ancient astronomy. But I think if we pause for a moment with the Hopewell, we may be able to see at least one way in which their enterprise in mound building was like the 1786 adventure in fort building. True, Fort Steuben was not built to study or reflect the alignment of the stars. But it was built for the protection and comfort of men who were indeed engaged in studying astronomical orientations—the surveyors. If we think of land surveyors simply as grunts who try to make straight lines on the ground, then we won't have a true picture of the surveyors who called Fort Steuben home in 1786 and 1787. Those men were scientists, though some may have been amateurs at the science. Measuring a straight line on the ground came later. First they had to do more or less what the Hopewell astronomers had done: find their position by the stars. As different as their objectives and their circumstances might have been, the Hopewell sages and the Fort Steuben surveyors were linked in a common humanity asking: where am I? How am I oriented toward the rest of the universe?

In quite another sense, the people who tried to rebuild Fort Steuben—not just at the end of the twentieth century but other, earlier attempts throughout the history of the town named after the fort—were asking those same questions, or similar ones. You don't start digging in the dirt for traces of your past unless the question of where you are, both in space and time, is important to you.

Fort Steuben as it may have looked in the spring of 1787; painting by Jess Hager, 1994.

Rebuilding your past requires a sense of place and how you got there—and who was there before you. So of course there is a place for the Adena people and the Hopewell in this story.

In our zeal to correct painful errors in the history of our nation, it is sometimes tempting to assume that the earliest white settlers across the Ohio were intent only on planting a flag or a farm, without a thought for the people who came before them. Also, because archaeology as a discipline was largely a product of the nineteenth century, a similar temptation might arise to deny the soldiers, surveyors and settlers of the 1780s any scientific imagination concerning the land they were occupying. This would be a mistake, especially when it comes to the men who built Fort Steuben. Colonel Harmar himself instructed his officers to take careful notes and even sketches of any signs of the antiquities of the ancient Americans. Captain Jonathan Heart, a Yale scholar who built Fort Harmar and for a brief time worked with some of the Fort Steuben surveyors, sketched the first published images of the Adena and Hopewell mounds, which appeared in the *Columbian Magazine* in May 1787.

In his 1885 biography of Heart, Consul Willshire Butterfield recorded that Lieutenant Ebenezer Frothingham, who served at Fort Steuben, collected even more extensive data on the prehistoric remains in Ohio. Unfortunately, however, and perhaps ironically, Frothingham's papers were never recovered from "Harmar's Defeat" of October 22, 1790, when Frothingham fell in battle with the Shawnee. On March 17, 1787, Harmar sent some of Heart's sketches to General Thomas Mifflin in Philadelphia in hopes that they would be passed on to Franklin's American Philosophical Society. "Be pleased to view the inclosed plan," he wrote, "of the remains of some ancient works on the Muskingum, taken by a Captain of mine, with his explanations. Various are the conjectures concerning these fortifications. From their regularity I conceive them to be the works of some civilized people. Who they were I know not."

We know a little more about the Adena and Hopewell than Harmar did, but not much. The Hopewell populated the Ohio Valley for seven centuries, from 200 BC until AD 500. How they disappeared, and who, if anyone, replaced them, is a mystery. There is no sign of war in the Hopewell remains, and any violence sufficient to obliterate these people would have left definite archaeological evidence. Native legend does have one clue to fill in the gaps between the Hopewell and the tribes who lived here in historical times. According to both Osage and Iroquois tradition, members of the Osage nation were long settled in the Ohio Valley when they were pushed west by

Ohio Before the Fort

Fort Steuben's logo: a sentry and a blockhouse.

the Iroquois about AD 1200, leaving the Ohio in the hands of the Iroquois, a confederacy of nations from central New York State. By the early days of the seventeenth-century Beaver Wars, however, about 1638, the Shawnee were attempting to settle the Ohio Valley. They were continually repulsed by the Iroquois, who did not live in the Ohio territory (or at least not in large numbers) but wanted it for hunting lands. So did the Wyandot, a Huron people pushed out of New York and Canada by the Iroquois. So did the Miami and the Lenape.

By that time (early to mid-1600s), the Europeans had also arrived. A century and a half later, they would be pushing west with a hunger for land that would make Fort Steuben necessary. In the seventeenth century, however, the hunger was for furs, the economic engine of French, English and Dutch claims west of the Ohio. That hunger drove the Beaver Wars, intertribal warfare over increasingly scarce natural resources. Each of the European nations enlisted Native Americans to drive out the others, and the result was a perpetual state of war in the second half of the seventeenth century. When the more than sixty years of warfare concluded with the Great Peace of Montreal in 1701, the Iroquois agreed to allow the Shawnee to settle in the upper Ohio Valley, though that resettlement took more than a generation. The first non-Iroquois nations to resettle the Ohio country were the Lenape (named "Delaware" by the English after the governor of Jamestown), who populated the lower Ohio Valley by 1720. By 1740, the Shawnee had returned to the upper Ohio, including the future home of Fort Steuben. About the same time, the Ottawa, an Algonquian-speaking nation related to the Lenape, settled along the Lake Erie shore. The Miami, another nation ousted by the Iroquois in the Beaver Wars, populated northwestern Ohio about 1750. The Huron rivals of the Iroquois, known in Ohio as the Wyandot, were in the northeast part of the state by mid-century.

As brief and basic as this sketch of eighteenth-century native migration is, it should at least be clear why the question "Who was here before the fort?" is not easy to answer. None of the native peoples who lived in Ohio at the time of the American settlement of the territory had been there very long.

And only a few years after the Lenape, Shawnee, Wyandotte and Miami had settled in Ohio, an outside war between two other nations—the French and the English—threatened to displace the various native people once again. In 1754, the conflict known to the English colonists as the French and Indian War erupted in the thirteen colonies. However, because the French fur trade now dominated the western frontier of the English colonies, the Ohio Valley became a dangerous place for native people to live. They were caught between two feuding European peoples. All of the Ohio Indians sided with the French in the conflict; a generation later, in the American Revolution, they would all side with the British against the Americans. At the conclusion of both wars, the Ohio nations found themselves allied with the losing side. No wonder, then, that Ohio Indians had so little negotiating leverage in the treaties of the 1780s that made possible the surveying of the Ohio country— the second beginning of the fledgling United States.

THE (SECOND) TREATY OF FORT STANWIX, 1784

The first attempt of the U.S. government to induce Native Americans to relinquish claims in Ohio was actually beneficial to Ohio's Indians— because it involved the Iroquois confederacy in New York. The nations that had pushed the Miami, the Shawnee, the Lenape and the Wyandot out of Ohio in the previous century still asserted a right to the land. That claim—certainly an indefensible one from a Shawnee or Lenape point of view—had been recognized by the English colonial government by the First Treaty of Fort Stanwix (present-day Rome, New York) in 1768. Worse, the Lenape war leaders Bemino (John Killbuck, Sr.) and Turtleheart, as well as Shawnee chief Benevissica, had watched what they considered their homeland being essentially deeded to the Iroquois by British soldiers.

The first Stanwix Treaty of 1768 was forgotten fifteen years later, when that same British army that had negotiated it (now defeated in the American Revolution) met in Paris to sign a peace treaty with the new United States. No Lenape, Shawnee, Miami or Wyandot were invited to Paris in 1783. British claims on the Ohio lands were mentioned in the negotiations: the Crown relinquished all claims there—but the people who lived there were ignored in the matter. On September 3, 1783, the treaty was signed, and the Americans went home. On January 14, 1784, the Continental Congress—at that time the only government America had, since there was still no constitution and no president—ratified the treaty and delegated a

Fort Steuben's southeast blockhouse in the snow. The winter of 1786–87 was a harsh one; the river froze over by November, and many soldiers were without shoes.

hero of the Revolution to carry it back to Paris. The soldier they appointed was Colonel Josiah Harmar, soon to be commander of the U.S. troops that built Fort Steuben.

When Colonel Harmar returned home in the spring of 1784, there was not much of an army to command in America. With the war over (if not yet paid for), many Americans saw no need for a standing army. Yet Congress knew that there was a need: cash poor, the United States was land rich—if it could settle some of the western lands the British had quitclaimed. To do that, it would have to treat with the neglected Lenape, Shawnee, Miami and Wyandot and cancel that 1768 British treaty with the Iroquois. On October 22, 1784, the U.S. Indian commissioners began the process at the site of the British treaty: Fort Stanwix in Oneida County, New York. Harmar did not gattend, but two of his soldiers who would later serve at Fort did. Lieutenant John Mercer and Ensign Mahlon Ford both signed the Second Treaty of Fort Stanwix, which would clear the way (after a few promotions) for *Captain* John Mercer and *Lieutenant* Mahlon Ford to help build Fort Steuben.

Ford and Mercer were not the only Fort Steuben personnel who signed the treaty, however. Among the six men who signed as witnesses was Samuel Montgomery, who in two years would seek the shelter of Fort Steuben while he surveyed the first seven ranges of Ohio. Also, the commissioner of Indian affairs, Richard Butler, who arranged the 1784 treaty, had several connections with Fort Steuben. First, he visited the surveyors on the line just before the fort was built. Second, he continued to send intelligence about Indian intentions in the Ohio Valley to Fort Steuben during the surveying. Finally, a bit less directly, he had a run-in with the fort's namesake at Yorktown. In the climactic battle of the Revolution, General George Washington had delegated to Butler, then a major, the honor of receiving British General Cornwallis's sword of surrender. Baron von Steuben thought it unseemly that a British general should surrender to a mere major and demanded to receive the sword himself. Only the diplomatic skills of Washington prevented a duel between Butler and the baron. Since this fort in the Ohio wilderness would be named after him, perhaps it would be good to know a little about this Prussian nobleman who helped win American independence. Who was this Steuben who gave his name to a fort?

DIGRESSION: THE BARON

Friedrich Wilhelm Augustus Heinrich Ferdinand, Baron von Steuben (1730–1794), was a Prussian officer under Frederick the Great of Prussia (after whom he was named) who later fought for the Americans in their war for independence from the British. In fact, it was von Steuben's instruction of Prussian military science to the American troops that helped them win the war. General George Washington's last official act as commander in chief of the Continental army was to write a letter of thanks to von Steuben, saying that without his aid, the Americans could not have won the war.

Young Friedrich grew up in the army. His father, Wilhelm Augustin von Steuben (1699–1783), was a career military officer; his mother, Elizabeth von Jagvodin, was a noblewoman who could claim descent from Charlemagne. By the age of sixteen, von Steuben had his own commission in Frederick the Great's army and saw action in the War of Austrian Succession and the Seven Years' War, receiving a wound in the Siege of Prague in May 1757. The Seven Years' War was also fought in North America, where it became popularly known as the French and Indian War. After that war, von Steuben was one of only thirteen Prussian officers selected to train personally with

Friedrich Wilhelm Augustus Heinrich
Ferdinand, Baron von Steuben (1730–1794);
portrait by Ralph Earl (1751–1801).

Frederick the Great. Twenty years later, that training would be handed on to American soldiers at Valley Forge.

One of the myths Americans cherish about their Revolution is that they beat one of the best-trained armies in the world by fighting Indian style, picking off the silly, vulnerable, straight lines of redcoats from the cover of rocks and trees. But, in fact, the opposite is the case. Americans were losing badly with that style of fighting, because the barrage of lead from volleys of perfectly synchronized rows of firelocks was the most efficient way of utilizing that particular weapon. The perfectly timed movement of rows of soldiers looks impressive, but it was also functional. Movements had to be precise if one line was to get out of the way before the next line fired. Until the Americans learned to fight in this way—and the Prussians were the best in the world at it—they would not be able to stop the British infantry.

Benjamin Franklin met von Steuben in Paris in 1777 and was impressed by the baron's résumé. Perhaps too impressed: because of a mistranslation, Franklin reported von Steuben to Washington as a Prussian "Lieutenant General"—a much higher rank than von Steuben ever held. Some biographers have accused von Steuben of fraud, exaggerating both his rank and his nobility. But recent research by Paul Douglas Lockhart has confirmed his right to the title "baron," and the American Continental army—as well as his military service to his new country—gave him the right to the rank of general.

Congress appointed von Steuben inspector general, and he began his work by training an elite corps of 120 men at Valley Forge, who in turn trained the rest of the army. His bayonet training allowed the Americans to win the Battle of Stony Point, which von Steuben commanded, with unloaded rifles. Steuben was present at the surrender of British general Cornwallis at Yorktown and can be seen in the famous painting of the event.

In addition to having an Ohio fort named after him, Steuben has received many honors from his adopted country (he became a citizen in 1783). On his 200th birthday in 1930, the U.S. Post Office issued a two-cent commemorative stamp with his likeness. In 1910, Albert Jaegers sculpted a monument of von Steuben for Lafayette Park (named after another foreign guy who fought in our Revolution) in Washington, D.C. There are also von Steuben statues in New York City, at Valley Forge and in front of the German Embassy in Washington. In Germany, there are two statues of von Steuben: one in his hometown of Magdeburg and one in Potsdam. The one in Potsdam was one of the first to go back up after the fall of the Berlin Wall. The Communist government in East Germany had taken it down to keep any connection with America away from German eyes. But with freedom, the people wanted the old Prussian back.

The author, as Baron von Steuben, drills some raw recruits at the Ohio Valley Frontier Days, June 2009.

In 2002, the PBS cartoon series *Liberty's Kids* ran a few episodes with the character of Baron von Steuben, voiced by actor and politician Arnold Schwarzenegger. In the First World War, a captured German ship was renamed the USS *Von Steuben*. Half a century later, a second USS *Von Steuben* (SSBN-632), a James Madison class fleet Polaris Missile submarine, was commissioned.

The baron's connection with the fort on the Ohio is not direct. Whenever I don the wig and visit schools or civic groups, one of the first questions, usually from the kids, is, "When was the baron here?" Alas, Baron von Steuben never visited the fort that took his name. But he knew it was there. In the late summer of 1786, when the troops sent to protect the surveyors gathered at Mingo Bottom, it was the baron's former aide-de-camp, Major William North, who met them there. It was he who informed the baron, in the spring of 1787, that there was a Fort Steuben on the Ohio, and the old Prussian was pleased.

MORE TREATIES: MCINTOSH (1785) AND FINNEY (1786)

With Iroquois claims to the Ohio lands now defunct, Butler and Harmar invited the Ohio nations to the home base of Harmar's First American Regiment, Fort McIntosh. The Shawnee, angry at their shabby treatment in previous negotiations and aware that their homeland lay closest to the region the U.S. government hoped to sell, refused to attend. But warriors of the Wyandot, Lenape, Ojibwe (sometimes called Chippewa) and Ottawa arrived. The Ojibwe did not have territorial stake in Ohio, but they were allied with the Ohio nations and feared that the Americans who wanted to settle in Ohio would not stop there but continue west into Ojibwe hunting grounds in Michigan, Wisconsin and Minnesota. Those fears, of course, were well justified and would soon become a reality.

In the negotiations that led to the treaty of January 21, 1785, at Fort McIntosh—thirty miles down the Ohio from Fort Pitt and about the same distance the other way from the future Fort Steuben—there is plenty for Americans to be ashamed of. The very naming of the parties in the treaty was a bit disingenuous. "The Commissioners Plenipotentiary of the United States of America"—that was clear enough: that meant Butler, George Rogers Clark (who a generation later would lead the "Voyage of Discovery" across most of the American West) and Arthur Lee. But the second party was named as "the Sachems and Warriors of the Wiandot, Delaware, Chippawa, and Ottawa Nations." Warriors of all those tribes attended and signed the treaty. But none of them was a "sachem," or chief, except for the Delaware leader Konieschquanoheel, known to the Americans as Hopocan, or "Captain Pipe." Some of the Ohio tribesmen later claimed that the ones who signed did not represent them and had been coaxed by drink into signing, even though alcohol was officially prohibited from treaty councils.

Nevertheless, if we can assume at least some of the American officials—at least Butler and Clark, who shared a mutual trust with the Ohio Indians—operated in good faith, there are at least two points in the McIntosh Treaty that are favorable to the Indians (though Congress did not pretend to be even-handed: it continually reminded the nations that the United States was the victor in a war that had ended with the Native Americans siding with the British). First, the boundaries of the land to be surveyed by the United States were drawn at what the commissioners determined to be the actual settlements of Wyandot, Lenape and Ottawa (Articles III–IV); the Shawnee were not represented, and the Ojibwe were there merely to affirm that they had no Ohio settlements. Second, and this was essential to the Fort Steuben soldiers' mission in the Ohio Valley, the U.S. government placed any squatters—Americans or Europeans on Indian lands—under Indian justice. The language was unambiguous: "If any citizen of the United States, or other person not being an Indian, shall attempt to settle on any of the lands allotted to the Wiandot and Delaware nations in this treaty, except on the lands reserved to the United States in the preceding article, such person shall forfeit the protection of the United States, and the Indians may punish him as they please" (Article V).

As commander of the western army, Colonel Harmar would be responsible for enforcing that article, and he signed the treaty as a witness. Another witness, one of Harmar's lieutenants, James Bradford, would be one of the officers who carried out Harmar's orders at Fort Steuben. A third was not in Harmar's army but would help it tremendously at Fort Steuben: Andrew van Swearingen, a Virginia frontiersman well known to Ohio Indians. We will hear more of him later.

Butler and Clark knew that peace in Ohio would not be possible without treating with the Shawnee, and the Shawnee response to the Treaty of Fort McIntosh was immediate. They sent a black wampum belt, signifying war, to the commissioners. Butler negotiated carefully for the better part of a year, and on the last day of January 1786, he concluded a treaty with the Shawnee at Fort Finney, near modern-day Cincinnati. Even though the

Sally port, pickets and northeast blockhouse, looking up from Ohio Route 7 in 2006. The sign has been updated and the sally port replaced by the guardhouse.

Shawnee had boycotted the McIntosh Treaty, it had provided for Shawnee lands in western Ohio. The Shawnee objected to the geography, claiming the Ohio River as their border. But the U.S. commissioners finally succeeded in getting "Shawanoe" signatures on the Treaty of Fort Finney, placing Shawnee lands "at the south line of the lands allotted to the Wiandots and Delaware nations, at the place where the main branch of the Great Miami, which falls into the Ohio, intersects said line" (Article VI).

Like those of Stanwix and McIntosh, the Finney Treaty expressly warned U.S. citizens not to trespass on Indian lands thus defined. "If any citizen or citizens of the United States, shall presume to settle upon the lands allotted to the Shawanoes by this treaty, he or they shall be put out of the protection of the United States" (Article VII). Unfortunately for the Ohio Indians, U.S. citizens had "presumed" to settle on disputed lands even before the smoke from the Revolution cleared. These trespassers were scarcely less of a nuisance to the United States, however, not only because the presence on the Ohio side of the river threatened peace with the Indians, but also because the federal government had counted on the sale of Ohio lands to pay its vast war debt.

So when Colonel Harmar's troops were sent into the Ohio wilderness in the 1780s, they were not marching against the Musquaconocah and the

Tetebockshicka and the Konieschquanoheel of the Ohio Valley but the Charles Norrises and the John Rosses and John Castlemans. They were taking arms against the squatters.

THE SQUATTERS

Even before the Stanwix Treaty, Congress had strived to compel squatters out of the "Indian" side of the Ohio. Until the Constitutional Convention, which would not begin until Fort Steuben had been decommissioned, America operated under the Articles of Confederation, begun even before the Declaration of Independence and ratified as the law of the land in the United States on March 1, 1781, five months before the British surrender at Yorktown. But even then, in the midst of the War for Independence, some of our founders were anticipating the squatter problem. Article 9 of the Articles of Confederation includes this clause: "The United States in Congress assembled have the sole and exclusive right and power of regulating the trade, and managing all affairs with the Indians, not members of any of the states, provided that the legislative right of any State, within its own limits, be not infringed or violated."

On September 22, 1783, less than three weeks after the Treaty of Paris was signed, Elias Boudinot, who held the title "President of the United States in Congress" (yes, in a sense there were American presidents before George Washington), used the Indian clause of Article 9 as a warrant for enacting an official prohibition of settling beyond the original thirteen colonies without Congressional approval. The proclamation ran:

> *Whereas it is essential to the welfare and interest of the United States as well as necessary for the maintenance of harmony and friendship with the Indians, not members of any of the states, that all cause of quarrel or complaint between them and the United States, or any of them, should be removed and prevented: Therefore the United States in Congress assembled have thought proper to issue their proclamation, and they do hereby prohibit and forbid all persons from making settlements on lands inhabited or claimed by Indians, without the limits or jurisdiction of any particular State, and from purchasing or receiving any gift or cession of such lands or claims without the express authority and directions of the United States in Congress assembled.*

The tools that built Ohio. These are from the quartermaster's store at Fort Steuben, but similar ones built the many squatters' cabins destroyed by the soldiers between 1785 and 1787.

To the families already settled in the upper Ohio Valley—including at least three on the grounds where Fort Steuben would soon be built—the final clause of the proclamation was most chilling: "And it is moreover declared, that every such purchase or settlement, gift or cession, not having the authority aforesaid, is null and void, and that no right or title will accrue in consequence of any such purchase, gift, cession or settlement." Congress was telling Ohio settlers that their presence west of the river was illegal and their properties would be seized without compensation. They would be removed by force.

The ensuing year, 1784, kept Congress occupied mostly with plans for surveying the lands "North and West of the Ohio"—a cumbersome phrase soon to be simplified to "the Northwest Territory." But that's the surveyor's story. The squatters in that time were digging in—and mostly indulging in what are still an American's two favorite pastimes: going about their business and ignoring the authority of Congress.

All along the upper Ohio, farms began to spring up on the Ohio side. Starting from Fort McIntosh and going downriver toward the site of Fort

Steuben, Harmar's soldiers saw a farm at the mouth of Beaver Creek and another at Yellow Creek (the family names of both are unfortunately unrecorded). Continuing south, they found the families of Abraham Cronen, Jeremiah Stanbury and James Fay at what would today be Toronto, Ohio. Below them, on a second rise above the river, where Fort Steuben would stand two years later, the families of John and Martha Castleman, John Boley and David Waddle had built cabins. Two miles downriver was an old Mingo village where John Ross was trying to farm, and below him (present-day Rayland, Ohio), Charles Norris was starting a settlement.

On January 24, 1785, just three days after the signing of the McIntosh Treaty placed the squatters under Indian jurisdiction, the commissioners of Indian affairs ordered Colonel Harmar to send troops down the Ohio to evict all of these families. Since the surveying would have to wait until spring, Harmar did not order his troops out until March. In the meantime, Harmar sent Ensign John Armstrong to post warnings with all Virginia magistrates and all public places on the Ohio border, warning citizens not to attempt to settle on the Ohio lands until Congress had them surveyed and sold. Armstrong wrote Harmar from Wheeling:

> *I have, sir, taken some pains to distribute copies of your Instructions, with those from the Honorable the Commissioners for Indian Affairs, into almost every settlement west of the Ohio and had them posted up at most public places on the east side of the river, in the neighborhood through which those people pass. Notwithstanding they have seen and read those Instructions, they are moving to the unsettled countries by forties and fifties.*

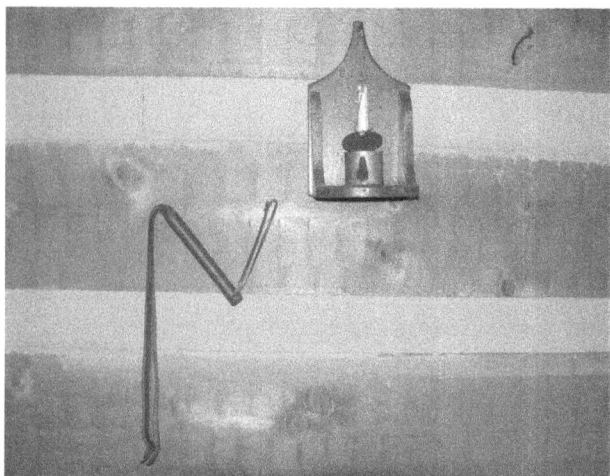

The cat-o'-nine-tails on Captain Hamtramck's wall is a reminder that Baron von Steuben's training manual prescribed lashings for various military infractions.

Meanwhile, the squatters were also organizing. While Congress was working as quickly as possible to settle the Northwest Territory methodically, some squatters, taking a page from the book of the American battle for independence, had dreams of starting their own states. On March 12, a ringleader named John Emerson posted advertisements all along the Virginia side of the Ohio, wherever would-be squatters would pass over to the Ohio country (that is, wherever Armstrong had posted his warnings from Congress), announcing a plan to elect leaders for a new territorial government without any legal tie to the United States:

> *ADVERTISEMENT.*
> *March 12, 1785*
>   *Notice is hereby given to the inhabitants of the west side of the Ohio river that there is to be an election for the choosing of members of the convention for the framing a constitution for the governing of the inhabitants, the election to be held on the 10th day of April next ensuing,* viz.: *one election to be held at the mouth of the Miami river, and one to be held at the mouth of the Scioto river, and one on the Muskingum river, and one at the dwelling house of Jonas Menzon, the members to be chosen to meet at the mouth of the Scioto, on the twentieth day of the same month.*
>   *I do certify that all mankind, agreeable to every constitution formed in America, have an undoubted right to pass into every vacant country, and there to form their constitution, and that from the confederation of the whole United States, Congress is not empowered to forbid them, neither is Congress empowered from that confederation to make any sale of the uninhabited lands to pay the public debts, which is to be by a tax levied and lifted by authority of the legislature of each state.*

Whether Emerson was right that Congress was not "empowered to forbid" squatters from settling west of the Ohio might have made fascinating philosophical and legal wrangling, but the "empowerment" arm of Congress was Harmar's First American Regiment—and they were ready to bet their muskets against the arms of the squatters to try the case in a more practical court than that of abstract opinion.

The detachment sent by Harmar was absurdly small considering the numbers of the Ohio squatters. Armstrong reported seeing crowds of American settlers all down the Ohio and its tributaries, "upwards of three hundred families" at the falls of the Hockhocking, three hundred more along the Muskingum and more than fifteen hundred on the Miami and

The Veterans' Memorial Fountain at the Eastern Gateway Visitor's Center welcomes visitors to Fort Steuben—and to all of the Ohio Valley.

Scioto Rivers. Against this tide of immigration, Armstrong marched with twenty soldiers and fifteen days' provisions. Leaving McIntosh on March 31, they crossed Beaver Creek the following day, destroying one family's cabin there. Four miles below Beaver, Armstrong found several families living in shacks, but since they had no raft for crossing back to the Virginia side, the ensign gave them until the end of April to vacate. At Yellow Creek, the soldiers burned another two cabins, and reaching the Castleman-Boley-Waddle settlement on April 3, they set fire to all the buildings.

By now, some of the squatters were beginning to rethink their defiance of Congress—yet others prepared to dig in. Boley, who was a native of Pittsburgh, simply hid out there for a while. He would return one more time, only to be evicted again, before moving to the Illinois country, where in 1803 he met Lewis and Clark and signed on with their expedition of discovery. But the Castlemans stayed near their homestead and decided to challenge Congressional authority, filing a grievance on April 11, 1785. John, his son Andrew and his brother Jacob signed the complaint, protesting forced removal and the burning of their homes.

Farther downriver, however, more direct opposition heated up. At Mingo, Joseph Ross challenged the army's authority. First he expressed doubt that Armstrong's orders were really from Congress, and then he decided to defy Armstrong on more practical grounds, voicing the uncomfortable truth that Congress could not possibly police the frontier. If Armstrong destroyed his cabins, Ross said, he would build six more as soon as they retreated. And this is more or less what happened in the ensuing year. For now, however, when Armstrong's men overpowered Ross, clapped him in irons and marched him off under guard to Wheeling, the remaining men in Ross's settlement capitulated, and Armstrong gave them a few days to clear out.

By now, word of the advancing soldiers had continued downriver. On the night of April 4, Charles Norris led a militia of armed men into Armstrong's camp and demanded to see the ensign's orders from Congress. Following John Emerson's example of territorial organization, people in the settlement below Mingo—what would now be Rayland, Ohio—had elected Norris justice of the peace and named the settlement Norris Town. This would-be peace officer deputized several men and met Armstrong's detachment with loaded muskets. The Norris party must have been outnumbered, for they surrendered their weapons and returned unarmed to Norris Town but warned Armstrong that the settlement was still heavily armed and that his men had been instructed to resist the soldiers.

The next day, April 5, Armstrong's full force arrived at Norris Town and asked to parlay with Norris. He told Norris that if the settlers resisted, the soldiers would fire on them. Again, Norris defied the ensign. Armstrong drew his sword and called out the commands from Baron von Steuben's manual of arms: "Half-cock—Firelock!" The locks of twenty muskets clicked. "Handle—Cartridge!" Twenty right hands entered twenty cartridge boxes, and each brought a cartridge up to a soldier's teeth—such teeth as they had. A man without at least two teeth, an upper and a lower in close enough proximity to connect, was ineligible for the U.S. Army in 1785 for this very reason. Twenty sets of teeth ripped open the cartridge—simply a packet of paper enclosing a pre-measured charge of gunpowder. "Prime!" Twenty right hands emptied the powder into the pan, but this was enough for the Norris party. They dropped their weapons and signaled their surrender to Armstrong, who ordered his men to stand down. The "Battle of Norris Town" was not to be.

Reenactors fire muskets during the Ohio Valley Frontier Days (formerly Fort Steuben Festival), held every June.

Ensign Armstrong gave the party until April 19—two weeks—to abandon Norris Town. After the ordeal, on April 12, Armstrong wrote to Colonel Harmar, "It is the opinion of many sensible men (with whom I convened on my return from Wheeling) that if the Honorable the Congress do not fall on some speedy method to prevent people from settling on the lands of the United States west of the Ohio, that country will soon be inhabited by banditti, whose actions are a disgrace to human nature."

Armstrong's courage in facing the muskets of Norris Town is even more amazing when we consider that he could not even be sure there would still be a U.S. Army. The resolution that had raised the army had now expired, and Congress on April 7—two days after the showdown at Norris Town—called on Lieutenant Colonel Harmar to raise a new army. Soldiers already serving could, of course, reenlist. But the order would not be executed until the end of that summer. Worse, at least for morale, was the reduction of officer's pay by Congress a few days later, on April 12. Until he knew if he would have an army to command, Harmar would send no more troops to evict squatters.

Congress proposed an army of 700 men: 165 each from New York and Connecticut and 110 from New Jersey. The remaining 260 were up to Colonel Harmar to recruit from Pennsylvania. On May 24, Harmar sent a list of 14 officers currently serving who were willing to make the three-year commitment to guard the Ohio frontier. Of those 14, 3 would see service at Fort Steuben: in addition to Ensign Armstrong, Lieutenant Ekuries Beatty, who would be the paymaster of the western army, and Captain William McCurdy, who would command one of three Fort Steuben companies. Still, as late as June 1, Harmar was writing to John Dickinson, Congressional delegate and president of Pennsylvania: "In consequence of the resolution of Congress of the 7th of April last, I am daily expecting instructions from your Excellency and the Honorable Council to discharge the men, and to re-enlist for three years such as are willing to serve."

By September, Harmar had received his orders and prepared another raid on the squatters. General Butler, the Indian commissioner, had to descend the Ohio on his way to further tribal negotiations, so he warned every settler on the Ohio side of the impending raids. He had a young colonel with him, recently elected to Congress, named James Monroe—later the fifth president of the United States. Butler described Monroe as "a member of Congress from the State of Virginia, a gentleman very young for a place in that honorable body; but a man well read, very sensible, highly impressed with the consequence and dignity of the federal Union, and a determined supporter of it in its fullest latitude."

Butler's journal records the names of three families he warned off in the Fort Steuben region: a Jesse Penniman just below Yellow Creek; a man named Pry below that; and Armstrong's old friend Joseph Ross at Mingo. Butler's journal shows no awareness of Ross's arrest six months earlier. He recorded on October 1:

> We got aground, as did six boats; passed on to the Mingoe towns, where we found a number of people, among whom one Ross seems to be the principal man of the settlers on the north side of that place. I conversed with him, and warned him and the others away. He said he and his neighbors were misrepresented to Congress; that he was going to Congress to inform them that himself and neighbors were determined to be obedient to their ordinances, and we had made it a point to assure them that Congress had no respect to persons, that the lands would be surveyed and sold to poor and rich, and that there would, or could be no more of preference given to one more than another, which seemed to give satisfaction.

Fort Steuben from the riverbank. The Sally port, shown here, would be replaced by the guardhouse in 2009–10.

The ease with which the squatters, outnumbering soldiers on the frontier something like fourteen to one, avoided or confronted the soldiers convinced Harmar that the army needed permanent bases of operations for mounting raids on the squatters. The need was particularly urgent after May 20, 1785, when Congress passed the first of several ordinances for the surveying and settling of land beyond the Ohio. Fort Pitt, which had become the base of operations for the western army, was clearly too far upriver to protect the frontier. McIntosh, thirty miles downstream, was not much better. The army spent the summer looking for likely spots for new forts while United States geographer Captain Thomas Hutchins assembled a survey team. In September, an artillery company under Captain David Doughty, later joined by an infantry company under Captain Jonathan Heart, built a pentagonal stockade near the mouth of the Muskingum. The fort, near what would soon be Marietta, was named after the commander of the western army, Lieutenant Colonel Josiah Harmar.

A few weeks later, on September 29, 1785, twelve keelboats carrying a company of soldiers (about seventy men, including engineers) left McIntosh under the command of Captain Walter Finney, bound for the mouth of the Miami on the Indiana border. This expedition made slower progress,

The twenty-first-century Steubenville skyline peeks over the eighteenth-century roofs of Fort Steuben.

not reaching the Miami until October 22, but it soon erected a second fort, which the men named for their captain—Fort Finney. These two forts would become the center of army activity on the frontier for the next five years; Fort Harmar became Colonel Harmar's headquarters immediately. From Fort Harmar would issue most of the orders that governed the construction and administration of Fort Steuben.

After wintering the army at these two forts, Harmar ordered another sweep of the Ohio, a year to the day after Armstrong's raid. Colonel Harmar did not send Armstrong this time but instead one of his captains, thirty-two-year-old John Francis Hamtramck—the man who would build and command Fort Steuben. Hamtramck, a French Canadian of Belgian ancestry, had grown up among French fur traders in what would become the Northwest Territory. His conflicts with the British made him sympathetic to the American cause, and he was commissioned by New York as a captain in the American Revolutionary forces in 1775. With a larger force than Armstrong's, Hamtramck destroyed nearly three dozen houses. Despite their complaint to Congress the year before, the Castlemans had returned and were once more evicted; at Norris Town, Hamtramck recorded the destruction of the cabins of William Huff, John McDonald, John Davis, Peter Street, Jonas Manser, James Dorothy and John Litton. The raid was a short-term success, but the army of course could not hold back the tide of immigration to the Ohio country. The new territory needed to be surveyed, and quickly.

THE SURVEYORS

"Fort Steuben was built to protect the surveyors." That's the sound-bite summary, and it is about as true as most simple statements on complex issues. That is, it will hold up okay as long as you don't breathe on it too hard. The fact is, the surveyors were hard at work on the Seven Ranges long before the soldiers got there, and when the troops were initially dispatched to the area, it was, as we have seen, to evict squatters, not to escort surveyors. The many nameless axe-men and chain-men who did the grunt work were unskilled labor hired on the spot or along the way, but the surveyors were highly trained scientists, public officials sent by each of the thirteen states to survey enough land to retire the debt of each state from the War for Independence. Because they were public figures, we know at least a little bit about each of them. Perhaps the best way of getting to know Fort Steuben is getting to know the surveyors it protected.

The leader of the survey was the first geographer of the United States—in fact the only one, since the title changed in 1796—Thomas Hutchins. He was much older than any of the other Ohio surveyors, having been born the same year as Baron von Steuben (1730). Hutchins had explored the Ohio Valley before any of the officers of Fort Steuben were born. Born in New Jersey, Hutchins was orphaned at an early age and immigrated to the Ohio frontier (on the Virginia side) at age sixteen. His formative years were spent on the banks of the Ohio, and surely at least part of that time on the "Indian" side—modern-day Ohio. His knowledge of Native American customs made him valuable to the British army just beginning to secure a foothold against the French in the American West. In 1755, he became an Indian agent for the trader George Croghan, a job that required Hutchins to live among the various nations of Ohio Indians for two years.

In 1757, Hutchins was commissioned ensign in the Second Pennsylvania Regiment. Mind you, this was the *British* army: the Declaration of Independence was nearly twenty years in the future. Hutchins was the quartermaster at Fort Pitt when it was first built, and it was there that the colonial brass first noticed his extraordinary skill in drafting and geometric calculations. As quartermaster, he had to arrange supplies in a wilderness where trade routes were Indian trails, and General John Forbes asked Hutchins to map them. These were the early days of the French and Indian War, which pitted British colonial forces against the French and their Native American allies. Across the Atlantic, a young Baron Friedrich Wilhelm von Steuben was fighting in another front of the same war, known in Europe as the Seven Years' War. In the last of those seven years, the autumn of 1764, Hutchins rode with Colonel Henry Bouquet into the Ohio country, reaching the Tuscarawas River and drawing, in the process, the first accurate map of Ohio, published in 1765. The following year, 1766, he floated the entire length of the Ohio from its source at the confluence of the Allegheny and Monongahela (Pittsburgh) to the Mississippi.

By the time he was tapped by Congress to be the United States geographer and lead a team of surveyors into the American wilderness, Hutchins had seen (and mapped) probably more of America than any other human being—as far west as Minnesota and as far south as New Orleans. In 1788, he produced a plan, which he unfortunately did not live to execute, for a

Soldier's-eye view of the garrison flag at Fort Steuben.

two-year exploratory mission to the Pacific—fifteen years before Lewis and Clark's voyage of discovery.

Hutchins had been part of Andrew Ellicott's boundary commission that had finished what Mason and Dixon had left undone: the rest of the southern boundary of Pennsylvania and the entire western boundary. The Land Ordinance passed by Congress on May 20, 1785, defined the starting point of the Seven Ranges—the very first expansion of the United States beyond the original thirteen states—as "on the river Ohio, at a point that shall be found to be due north of the western termination of a line, which has been run as the southern boundary of the state of Pennsylvania." Two curious points of grammar lie in that "shall": first, it denotes a command. Second, it implies *future*: "shall be found to be" meant that on May 20, 1785, the northwest boundary of Pennsylvania had not yet been determined. But exactly three months later, on August 20, Ellicott and Hutchins placed a wooden post to mark the spot. There is now a granite marker bearing this inscription:

1112 FEET SOUTH OF THIS SPOT WAS THE "POINT OF BEGINNING" FOR SURVEYING THE PUBLIC LANDS OF THE UNITED STATES. THERE, ON SEPTEMBER 30, 1785, THOMAS HUTCHINS, FIRST GEOGRAPHER OF THE UNITED STATES, BEGAN THE GEOGRAPHER'S LINE OF THE SEVEN RANGES. THIS INSCRIPTION WAS DEDICATED SEPTEMBER 30, 1960, IN JOINT ACTION OF THE EAST LIVERPOOL HISTORICAL SOCIETY AND THE AMERICAN CONGRESS ON SURVEYING AND MAPPING.

Hardly anyone knows the marker is there. Hardly anyone knows how important it was.

The curators of Independence Hall in Philadelphia, thinking of the signing of the Declaration, might be able to claim "America began here," if by "America" is meant the original thirteen states. But the *rest* of America began right at Ellicott's post, the "point of beginning," and from that point on the job belonged to Hutchins. As U.S. geographer, Hutchins called in thirteen deputies, one from each state, to begin the Seven Ranges (the Land Ordinance had specified seven). Only eight states complied: New Hampshire sent Edward Dowse; Massachusetts, Benjamin Tupper; Connecticut, Isaac Sherman; New Jersey, Absalom Martin; New York, William Morris; Virginia, Alexander Parker; Maryland, James Simpson; and Georgia, Robert Johnston (who was actually from Baltimore).

This team began September 30 but only worked for a little over a week. About 3:00 p.m. on the afternoon of September 30, Indian commissioner

Ohio Before the Fort

This granite monument marks the "Point of Beginning" of the Seven Ranges—the first American land beyond the original thirteen states.

Butler arrived at the surveyors' camp on his way to bring gifts from Congress to the Indians, and Hutchins took the opportunity to express his apprehension over his vulnerability to attack. "I felt a little uneasiness," Butler confided to his journal, "on hearing Capt. H[utchins] mention that if the Indian chiefs did not come to him he would instantly quit the business and return, as he could not think himself and people safe. I conversed with Capt. M[ercer] a very sensible young gentleman; I gave him as my opinion, that they should go on as soon as the geographer had run a sufficient distance on the west line for them to begin, and that I felt confident the Indians would not attempt to injure them until they gave them warning; until which time I think it would betray a timidity that should not be shown by public officers."

Butler's belittling of the geographer's fears was a bit disingenuous, since the previous evening at Fort McIntosh he had met with a trader named Irvine who reported an attack below Wheeling by a pair of rogue Cherokee who killed a man named Doolan only nine days earlier (September 20).

They came to the door and knocked very early in the morning, the man rose out of bed and was shot through the door which broke his thigh; on his falling, the door was broke in by the Indians, who tomahawked him and two children;

37

the woman in fright lay still. They told her not to be uneasy, that they would not hurt her or the child she had in her arms, and desired she would not leave the house, as they would soon be back again, but did not intend to injure her; that they were Cherokees and would never make peace. She asked why they troubled her, that the Indians had made peace with Gen. Clark last fall; they said not they, that if they could meet Gen. Clark they would kill him also. He says he does not think the Indians mean to do any mischief generally, that it is a few banditti who are a collection of Cherokees, Shawanees, &c.

Finding no sympathy with the Indian commissioner, Hutchins continued the survey. The Land Ordinance of 1785 required that the geographers, who were after all trained scientists, run their survey lines by "true meridian," which means taking a sighting on Polaris and the sun rather than magnetic compass. This was very slow work, and the team was paid by the mile, not by the day—the princely sum of two dollars a mile at a time when the American dollar was losing value almost daily. By October 8, Hutchins had completed only four miles when word came that Indian councils at Tuscarawas, fifty

Northern entrance to Fort Steuben, looking south into the compound. The stone marker erected by the city a century earlier can be seen.

miles west, were calling for attacks on the surveyors. The team retreated to Fort Pitt immediately, and the work was over for the year. One four-mile line, with no land ready for sale.

The following spring, however, Congress relented and on May 9 and 12, 1786, passed resolutions suspending the true meridian requirement and allowing the quicker, but less accurate, magnetic compass readings to run the survey. The stage was now set for the Fort Steuben moment: the actual survey of the Seven Ranges. The cast had changed slightly, however: Benjamin Tupper had returned to Boston after the Indian scare of 1785 and regaled his friends with tales of the rich Ohio lands. On January 10, 1786, Tupper and his friend, Revolutionary War general Rufus Putnam, placed ads in the Boston papers asking for investors in a land company. Three months later, on March 3, investors selected from the respondents met at the Bunch-of-Grapes Tavern and formed the Ohio Company of Associates. One of the associates, Winthrop Sargent, replaced Dowse as the New Hampshire geographer, and Ebenezer Sproat took over for Georgia's Johnston. Also, three states that had been no-shows the previous year came through in 1786: Pennsylvania sent Adam Hoops, North Carolina sent Samuel Montgomery and South Carolina sent Israel Ludlow. These eleven men would be the "gentlemen surveyors" known to the soldiers of Fort Steuben.

The geographers were ordered to convene at Fort Pitt in the summer of 1786. Hutchins arrived first, on July 8; the other surveyors arrived over the next few days, and on July 14, the surveyors floated down the Ohio from Fort Pitt. Camping at Fort McIntosh that night, they continued downriver the next day, reaching their previous year's camp on the afternoon of July 15. Smarting from Congressional displeasure at the poor showing the previous year, Hutchins took steps to ensure that all Seven Ranges requested by Congress would be run in 1786. To this end, he had the surveyors draw lots so that each geographer would be assigned a range.

"Range" is the term for a section of land in the rectilinear system of land measurement. One could almost say (in fact, many *have* said) that Hutchins himself invented the system. It is probably more accurate to say that in the eighteenth century, it was an idea whose time had come. Near the end of the French and Indian War, Hutchins marched with Henry Bouquet, a Swiss native who became a British general in the war, and showed his facility with designing forts and encampments, as well as mapping the Ohio regions. In 1765, an account of the expedition was published anonymously. A century later, in 1868, Francis Parkman identified the author as Dr. William Smith of the College of Pennsylvania, editing Bouquet's regimental papers. But the section suggesting methods for the future settlement of the territory through which Bouquet marched was unmistakably Hutchins. It reads like a demonstration in geometry:

> LET us suppose a settlement to be formed for one hundred families, composed of five persons each, upon an average.
>
> LAY out upon a river or creek, if it can be found conveniently, a SQUARE of one thousand seven hundred and sixty yards, or a mile for each side.
>
> THAT Square will contain----------------------640 acres
>
> Allowing for streets and public uses-------------40 "
>
> To half an acre for every house ----------------50 "
>
> To one hundred lotts at five and half acres------550 "

In the summer of 1786, then, Hutchins was finally getting a chance to put into practice the method of township settlement that he had imagined more than twenty years earlier.

The bronze plaque on the concrete pillar marking Fort Steuben, erected by the City of Steubenville in 1913.

The starting point of the rectangular survey, defined by Congress as the intersection of the western border of Pennsylvania with the Ohio River, had been established and marked the previous spring. That was the site of the surveyors' camp. From there, a straight east–west line would be run into the wilderness. Every six miles from the "Point of Beginning," a direct north–south line—called a range line—would be run from the east–west line until it reached the Ohio. Each section was marked out in this way, bounded on the north by the "geographer's line"—the east–west line—on the east and west by range lines (except for the first range, whose eastern border is the Ohio River) and on the south by the river.

Hutchins and Absalom Martin had already run the first four miles of the geographer's line. Because of his contributions the previous year, Martin was granted the first range. The rest relied on the luck of the draw. The second range fell to Adam Hoops of Pennsylvania, the third to Isaac Sherman of Connecticut, the fourth to Ebenezer Sproat of Rhode Island, the fifth to Winthrop Sargent (a Bostonian but standing proxy for New Hampshire), the sixth to James Simpson of Maryland and the seventh to William W. Morris of New York.

On July 20, Hutchins and Martin went off into the woods to finish the east–west line where it had stopped the previous fall. Though the other surveyors did not follow them, the chainmen who held the Gunter chains, measuring distances and keeping the lines straight, did. So did the axe men who had to cut a "vista," or viewing corridor, through any tree or bush that stood in the way. On the morning after the first day of work, when no further deputies appeared, Hutchins sent a message back to camp that the other surveyors would be needed if they were to finish that season. Benjamin Tupper, on behalf of his fellow surveyors, sent back a polite but firm reply: "Made sensible, of the general ill temper of the Indians, from a variety of corroborating circumstances and their partial mischief which has resulted from that disposition, we think it is our duty to inform you, as well for the publick good as our present protection, that a body of Troops will be necessary, to cover us in our operations."

This polite refusal disguised as compliance actually worked to Hutchins's benefit, because he could use it to request the troops he had wanted all along and attribute the demand to his deputies. On July 22, Hutchins forwarded Tupper's letter to Harmar, along with a request for troops:

> *The truth of the Information on which they have founded their opinions, to me* [that is, what Tupper called the "general ill-temper of the Indians" in Ohio] *seems not to be doubted, but even if it was, as*

View of the southeast
blockhouse, from the
northwest blockhouse
of Fort Steuben.

*the Matter now stands, my operations are equally affected, as in either
case, I am deprived of their assistance.—The good of the service therefore
constrains one humbly to request that you will be pleased to order as soon as
possible such a number of Troops to cover the Surveyors as in your opinion
will be sufficient for their protection.*

Hutchins was aware that there was already a considerable number of soldiers
in the upper Ohio preparing for another raid on squatters. Captain John Mercer
had left Fort Pitt on July 8, the day Hutchins arrived, with a full company of
soldiers headed for McIntosh to run an Ohio raid. On July 12, Harmar ordered
Captain Hamtramck, then commanding McIntosh, to join his company with
Mercer's and a third under Captain William McCurdy, all three to bivouac at
Mingo as a base for patrolling the upper Ohio. These three companies would
be together for the next full year. They would become the men of Fort Steuben.

While the squatters were occupying the soldiers, however, the surveyors
remained in camp and would not help Hutchins on the line. It was now
that the surveyors who were also land speculators showed their divided
nature. When a whiskey trader bound for the Muskingum stopped in the
camp on July 19, Winthrop Sargent urged Hutchins to let him go along
with the man, since the survey could not resume until the soldiers arrived.
A few days earlier, two young men from Massachusetts had arrived with a
letter for Sargent from Manasseh Cutler, urging him to be looking for ideal
locations for the settlements of the Ohio Company of Associates. In a sense,
then, Sargent was allowing his orders from the Ohio Company to supersede
his orders from Congress and the Geographer's Department. Hutchins let

Sargent go. The would-be land baron left on July 20, and when he returned, on August 9, Hamtramck's troops had reached the camp.

Sargent's diary records his enthusiasm for the country through which he traveled but also a distaste for the squatters now deeply imbedded in the interior of Ohio. When he told them of his mission to survey the land—which the squatters thought of as theirs (an opinion the Shawnee, Lenape, Miami and Congress thought rather odd)—they were understandably disconcerted. But when he told them of the surveyors' apprehension over Indian violence, Sargent was shocked at the squatters' reaction. In the soldiers and surveyors, Indian violence inspired fear; in the squatters Sargent met, it inspired hatred, a hatred which Sargent labeled "insane." The sooner Ohio was settled with stable military veterans, the better.

THE SOLDIERS

Even as Sargent was writing that in his diary, some 150 military men—most of them veterans of the Revolution—had set up camp at "Mingo Bottom," from which they scoured the Ohio Valley of squatters. The importance of this mission—in addition to the fact that more than one-fifth of the entire U.S. Army was now here—was signaled by the presence of two of the federal army's top brass. The inspector general, Major William North, reviewed the troops on July 23, and the paymaster, Major Ekuries Beatty, brought them their pay on August 2. North had been aide-de-camp to the previous inspector general, Baron von Steuben, and it would be through Major North that the baron would learn of the fort named for him in the Ohio wilderness. Beatty would be a regular visitor to the region once Fort Steuben became headquarters for the three companies.

Two days after Beatty's visit, on August 4, an express message from Colonel Harmar ordered all three companies north to the surveyors' camp in response to Hutchins's request for protection. At the same time, Hutchins sought protection another way. Both Lenape and Chippewa (Ojibwe) sent delegations to Hutchins to determine his intentions, and Hutchins sent a request with a Lenape messenger named Turis for warriors or sachems to join the surveyors for their protection.

Captain Hamtramck marched his company north to the surveying camp on the Little Beaver, ordering Mercer and McCurdy to follow him with their companies. Hamtramck arrived on August 5, expecting to be met by a supply flotilla from Pittsburgh. It was not there. Nor did it arrive the

Original architectural drawing of a Fort Steuben blockhouse and pickets by architect Lester J. Zapor, 1989.

next day. Nor the next. Nor the one after that, August 8, when two more companies arrived, bringing the total number of soldiers in the camp to 150, with no food supplies. The army had contracted with Turnbull, Marmie and Company of Philadelphia, who had warehouses in Pittsburgh. Daniel Britt, the manager of the Pittsburgh office, had promised the army that he could supply the army anywhere on the Ohio. Over the coming year, Britt would have a great deal of trouble making good that claim, but this particular supply problem was not Britt's fault. As it turns out, it was the fault of one of Captain Hamtramck's fellow officers and would be the start of a great deal of friction between them—a sort of Fort Steuben soap opera.

After the first day of waiting, Hamtramck sent an express (which usually meant a fast horse over Indian trails) to Pittsburgh and also to the commander of Fort McIntosh, Captain William Ferguson, asking about the missing rations. But Britt was neither at Pittsburgh nor at McIntosh; he was delivering supplies to Indian agents on the Muskingum. McIntosh in 1786 was the key link in the supply chain of the western army; supplies from Pittsburgh contractors could easily be stored there for distribution on the frontier. That is why Colonel Harmar's order for supplies to Hamtramck's three companies—Hamtramck had a copy of it in his files—had been sent to Captain Ferguson at McIntosh.

Or so Hamtramck thought. Two days after sending indignant inquiries to the contractor and Ferguson, it occurred to Hamtramck to check with his own men to see what they knew about the supply order. What they knew, apparently, and what Hamtramck learned on August 8, was that the paper

This officers' kitchen at Fort Steuben has everything in it but food—which it was often without, due to the inability of contractor Daniel Britt to supply it.

was still in camp. It seems that Captain McCurdy had taken it from the messenger, saying that he "expected to go to McIntosh one of this days and intended to be the bearer." "One of this days" is Hamtramck's spelling; after a decade in an English-speaking army, Hamtramck still wrote with a Belgian–French Canadian accent.

Hamtramck was furious and wrote to Harmar to complain about McCurdy—the first of many complaints. But Hamtramck did not let the lack of food keep him from his duty. Reasoning that going hungry on the line is no worse than going hungry in camp, Hamtramck, on the morning of August 8, sent Lieutenant William Kersey, an unnamed sergeant, and thirty privates, along with a light supply of "besket" (that is, biscuit with a French accent), to the end of the east–west line, five miles into the woods, to cover two surveying teams under Hutchins and Martin.

In two days, the teams pushed the east–west geographer's line an additional mile. Reaching the six-mile point was a big psychological boost to the surveyors, because it meant that the northern border of the first range was now completed and Martin could begin running the first range line, south to the Ohio. On August 11, he did just that, while Hutchins continued west. The leapfrogging of the other teams began. As soon as word came to the camp at the mouth of the Little Beaver, second range geographer Adam Hoops went into the woods (with another detachment of thirty-two soldiers) to help Hutchins move the line across the top of the second range.

Hoops joined Hutchins on the east–west line on August 15. He had one advantage over the rest of the surveyors: the help of a twenty-one-year-old apprentice named John Matthews. Matthews had arrived in the geographer's camp on July 31, sent by his uncle, Revolutionary War general and Ohio Company shareholder Rufus Putnam. Matthews would become a major player at Fort Steuben—and in Ohio history—before he was done. He and Putnam joined Hutchins on the line and in seven days extended it to twelve miles, allowing Hoops and Matthews to turn south on August 22 to run the second range line. By this time, Isaac Sherman had taken over on the east–west line.

As quick as this progress was, Winthrop Sargent, as the fifth-range geographer, knew that he would not be needed immediately, so he made another exit from the camp, this time to Pittsburgh. While there is no doubt that a state geographer who is also a private land speculator has divided interests, Sargent's private interests were not necessarily detrimental to the federal cause. For one thing, the private capital he brought the project was definitely welcome in the face of the financial limitations of Congress. Congress was paying in paper money, the value of which was eroding daily. Worse, the government was buying up old soldiers' land vouchers at pennies on the dollar, which the soldiers were glad to sell because they doubted they would ever get the land those papers promised. Sargent, on the other hand, had brought real gold and silver from his investors in New England and took it to Pittsburgh to hire packhorses, drivers and chainmen. Sargent promised—and paid—a "half-Joe" (a Portuguese gold coin worth eighteen English shillings at the time) a month for the chainmen and drivers and thirty shillings a month for the horses.

Meanwhile, Hamtramck was still wrangling with the contractor. Britt was able to send two hundred pounds of bacon, which arrived on August 20—too little too late, but welcome nonetheless. Hamtramck immediately sent shares to the men on the line. Finally admitting his inability to supply the army with salt provisions, Britt hired two Virginia hunters to accompany the men on the line. One of them, Andrew van Swearingen, was well known on the frontier and had been a witness at the Fort McIntosh Treaty the year before. What he saw while hunting along the east–west line opened the eyes of the surveyors and soldiers there.

Neither the soldiers nor the surveyors had encountered any Indians, but that is scarcely surprising because the soldiers moved on the march with fife and drum, scarcely inconspicuous, and the surveyors proceeded by felling large trees, which do not fall silently. But a hunter must use stealth, and while van Swearingen was procuring venison for the soldiers, he surprised an Indian lookout and found other evidence that Indians had been following

Hunter Andrew van Swearingen supplied Fort Steuben soldiers with game, such as this deer hanging in the commissary's store.

the progress of the survey. "The number of their Tracks that are daily seen," Hutchins wrote to Hamtramck on August 27, "and one of the Indians having been discovered by Mr. Swearingham, a Hunter, the Day before yesterday [are] sufficient reason to apprehend that they see Us every Day."

The discovery of Indian spies and the weakness of the supply chain convinced Captain Hamtramck that he needed a secure base closer to the surveyors. With the east–west line now (August 29) stretching more than twenty-four miles and three teams now running range lines south (Sherman was well down the third range, and Ebenezer Sproat's company had just started the fourth range line on August 28), Hamtramck wanted to be able to get to each team quickly when their range lines met the river. So he began drawing up plans for a march downriver to look for a suitable location for a more permanent headquarters.

It may seem odd that an officer of Hamtramck's experience would have to "draw plans" for such a march. But even though most of the soldiers on the western frontier had seen military service in the Revolution and were, for that reason, very well trained by Inspector General Baron von Steuben, marching three companies through a wilderness was a relatively new experience. Hamtramck hadn't even marched three companies this far; he had marched one, and the other two had followed at different times. No one among the soldiers had experience marching 150 men through Ohio. But one person among the surveyors had done so. He had, in fact, written the book on it.

Or rather, part of a book. We have already seen that Hutchins was the most likely author of the part of General Bouquet's book on the

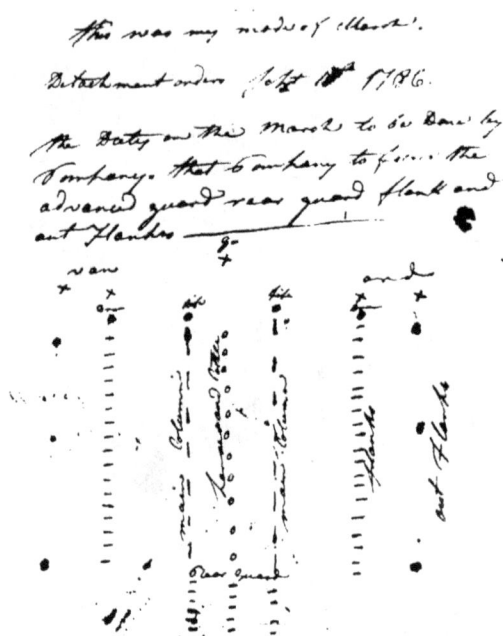

Hamtramck's order of march, issued September 1, 1786, but not executed until October 4. *Courtesy William L. Clements Library, University of Michigan.*

surveying of townships in new territories. But the section on marching large numbers of soldiers through the woods, while probably not written by Hutchins, was likely illustrated by him, prized as he was by Bouquet for his draftsmanship. Between pages 126 and 127 of *Historical Account of Bouquet's Expedition Against the Ohio Indians, in 1764* (Philadelphia, 1765) is an engraving labeled "Line of March" illustrating the movement of troops in the wilderness. Even if Hutchins did not draw it, he certainly knew it well, having been part of the expedition that conceived it; it is very likely that Hamtramck also had read the book and had seen the illustration. At any rate, his own sketch for his "Order of March" dated September 1, 1786, is very similar to that 1765 illustration.

For the next two months, in between their main work of protecting the surveying teams, Hamtramck's command practiced the march that would take the three companies and their supplies (when and if they arrived) downriver to their new headquarters—wherever that would be. In a letter to his commander, Colonel Harmar, Hamtramck gave a great deal of detail about the maneuver. "This was my mode of March," he wrote above his sketch of the troop placement. "Detachment orders Sept 1st 1786. the Duty on the March to be Done by Company. that Company to forme the advance guard rear guard flank and out Flanks." In other words, one of the three companies would supply the advance guard or vanguard (Hamtramck indicates this in the sketch by stretching out the word "vanguard": "van" in front of the left column, "gu" over the middle and "ard" over the right), as well as a guard on either side of the column (labeled "out flanks" in the sketch; Hamtramck only shows them on the right, but they would have been on the left as well) and rear guard. The central portion of the parade—two columns of soldiers flanking "horses and cattle"—would be made up of the other two companies.

Hamtramck's description of the march indicates the growing apprehension of Indian attack, occasioned not only by discovering the signs of the Indian observers but also by messages coming from traders and Indian commissioners who had visited the Shawnee and Lenape villages to the west of the surveyors. Hamtramck explained, with his Francophone spelling and haphazard eighteenth-century capitalization:

> *If atacked on the right Flank, the troops to face to the right and the left Column to move obliquely to the left, and on the Contrary if ataked to the left. If ataked in front or Rear all men to face outwards and the pack horses to forme in the rear. At the Beating of the long roll the troops to charge and Huza! the advanced guard at 400 y^d in front the troops in the path the main Columns and flank at 100 from each other the out Flank at 80 yd. from the flanks the Rear guard at 150 from the main body. I have performed the manoeuver it was very well done and quick—*

These practice sessions, however, had been without the horses and cattle. Hamtramck had sent Britt to Pittsburgh with an order for food supplies, twenty head of cattle and about thirty-five horses. "I have Calculated 7 men to a tent," Hamtramck wrote to Harmar, "and a horse for Every five tents, two for Every Company officer, and two for the Doctor and myself." The "Doctor" was Dr. John Elliott, Hamtramck's company surgeon, who had been with the group ever since deployment to Mingo Bottom. The extra horse for each officer was not a fresh mount but rather a packhorse for their personal effects—a luxury the enlisted men did not have. Dr. Elliott's packhorse, however, was not for luxuries but for his medical supplies, which, by eighteenth-century standards, was virtually a mobile field hospital. For an indication of what those might be, see the section following entitled "The Hospital."

While the soldiers prepared for their march, their need to move became more acute. On September 2, Indian agent Jacob Springer had returned to Fort McIntosh after visiting the Wyandot and Lenape villages at Lower

Sandusky on the Lake Erie shore, carrying a message from Hutchins. Hutchins was asking for those nations, as signatories of the Treaty of Fort McIntosh, to protect the surveyors. The response Springer brought with him was mixed, and it was carefully recorded in the regimental papers, a splendid example of Native American rhetoric. Springer had met with Wyandot chief Pomoacan, known in American documents as "Half King," and the Lenape leader Konieschquanoheel, known as "Captain Pipe" (*Hopocan* in Lenape). With Captain Pipe nodding in assent, this is what Half King said, as recorded in Harmar's papers:

> *My Friends and Brothers—*
> *We know what you all say, and Captain Pipe knows the same— you always tell me to let you know if the Southern Indians are for any mischief—Now I tell you for to take care of them, your people pass and repass through our Country and we never molest them—*
> *My Friends and Brothers*
> *Now Hold you my reason that the Chiefs cannot comply with your request to come and deliver up the lands for we are trying to bring the back Nations to terms (meaning the Otawas, Chipewas, Petawatamies and Miamies) as well as ourselves and we now hold a Council with them first before we can speak any with you concerning the abovementioned lands—*
> *My Brothers—*
> *If you would hold a Council with the back Nations it would be very much in your favor and likewise in ours for I am very much afraid that all we can say will be to little purpose with them—*
> *My Friends and Brothers—*
> *I am now just between two fires for I am afraid of you and likewise of the back Nations—*
> *My Brothers,*
> *If you have anything to say don't keep it in your hearts but let me know. You sent your friends here to me and I have heard all you had to say, and now I send four of my People back with him for fear of any accident might happen him on the way and then I would be to blame for it—Now my Brothers I send my People to you I expect you will take care of them and not let them be hurt*
> *Now my Friends and Brothers I take you by the hand—*

With this symbolic hand shake, Pomoacan gave Springer a belt of black and white wampum recording the essence of the speech.

Nineteenth-century foundation stones unearthed by the archaeological dig at Fort Steuben. Remains of the original fort continue to elude the archaeologists.

Pomoacan's assessment of the precarious situation could not have been more succinct. The Wyandot and Lenape would not bother the surveyors, but they did not speak for the "back Nations." The federal government was relying for its warrant in claiming the eastern Ohio lands—what Congress even before the start of the survey had begun calling the "Seven Ranges" of the "Northwest Territory"—on a document that did not represent the will of all of the Ohio nations. As for Hutchins's request for a Wyandot-Lenape escort or guarantee of safety, Pomoacan would send his four warriors, but it would only be a symbolic gesture. It would have no bearing on the "back Nations," and Pomoacan was clearly warning Hutchins: "Take care of them." Watch out.

With the message, Springer delivered his own assessment. Pomoacan was clear that he did not speak for the back nations, but a chafing fact that he did not express is that he did not even speak for all of his own nation. He was the leader, the "Half King," but many younger warriors thought of his policies as appeasement and wanted to hold the Americans at the Ohio River. Springer knew that the younger Wyandot and Lenape (Delaware) were ready to fight the Americans but felt confident that Pomoacan's generation could restrain them. "It is my opinion," he wrote to Hutchins, "that the Chiefs of the Wyandots & Delawares will not consent to their young men committing any hostilities upon the surveyors without first desiring them to leave off surveying." So there would be no attacks without warning from the treaty nations. But not all of the Indians in Ohio were from those nations. "What the Banditti consisting of about 200 Men composed of different Nations known by the names of the Cherokees and Mingoes may do I cannot take upon me to say," Springer concluded.

In addition to Springer's report, the surveyors were beginning to receive other reports of tension in the area. Simon Girty and George Brickell had visited the Shawnee towns south of Sandusky immediately after Springer's departure, and on September 3 they witnessed a war council. Brickell's deposition of September 13 stated that "there were seven hundred Indian Warriors assembled at the Shawano Towns, and that their numbers in a short time would be two thousand; that their intentions were to strike first at Wheeling settlement, & then lower down River." Girty's deposition reported that the Shawnee kept asking him "if Capt. Hutchins was come to own the land." Girty assured them that he was only measuring it for sale to others. Regardless, the Shawnee told Girty to warn Hutchins that they "meant to cut off him & all his men."

The essence of those middle weeks of September 1786 was rumors of war and hunger. The soldiers' diet was meager enough, despite the abundance of game and wild vegetables in the forest, simply because their military duties prevented them from hunting or foraging. Clearly, the building of a permanent home base was a key to both problems: the food supply chain and Indian attacks. One of the most frequent questions visitors to the reconstructed Fort Steuben ask is, "What did the soldiers eat?" In September 1786, just before the construction of Fort Steuben, the answer would have been, "not much." When Britt sent van Swearingen to hunt, the intended game was venison, but even in the military beggars were not choosers, and the troops on the Ohio were often moved to eat things they might have passed up at home. In his diary for September 12, Sargent records van Swearingen's take as being nothing but a panther and two turkeys, "scarcely more than a morsel to a man," though he admitted finding the panther delicious. Hunger makes the best sauce. The same scenario had been played out in the same woods nine months earlier (December 12, 1785), when a soldier unconnected with Hamtramck's companies, Major Ebenezer Denny, was rescued by Wheeling's Isaac Zane. Zane, in a rather unorthodox way, saved Denny from starving. "He killed a doe," Denny reported, "opened the udder with his knife—milk collected, of which I drank."

What a contrast to the picture of frontier dining Colonel Harmar had sent to fellow Colonel Francis Johnston just the previous June. "I wish you were here to view the beauties of Fort McIntosh. What think you of pike of 25 lbs.; perch of 15 to 20 lbs.; cat-fish of 40 lbs.; bass, pickerel, sturgeon, *etc., etc.*?" Despite Harmar's fish stories, however, even a forty-pound catfish would be less than one meal for a company—and Hamtramck had to feed three companies.

The last straw that forced Hamtramck to move his troops as he had been practicing since the first of September was an express from Fort

A soldier and a frontiersman swap stories during Ohio Valley Frontier Days, June 27, 2009.

McIntosh on September 18 reporting Shawnee war dances to the west. John Matthews met the rider with the report while working on the east–west line. Both Hamtramck and Hutchins were on the line at the time, so the colonel mustered his men for defense while the surveyors, scattered with Hamtramck's soldiers throughout the Seven Ranges, were recalled to their rendezvous at the geographer's "point of origin" at the mouth of Beaver Creek. Matthews, who had befriended many of the frontiersmen, retreated to the Virginia side of the river, where he was welcomed into the home of William Greathouse for the duration of the Indian scare.

Not all of the surveyors, and certainly none of the soldiers, were so comfortable. Many were well down the range lines, and some were even beginning to survey townships within the ranges. W.W. Morris came in from the seventh range and James Simpson (who had been lost in the woods for three days the week before) from the sixth. But on the fifth range, Winthrop Sargent had progressed so far south that the messenger did not reach him until September 20. And when he did reach the single-minded surveyor, he was unable to convince Sargent that the alarm was anything more than a rumor or frontier jitters. "I am very much of opinion," Sargent told his diary, "that this is a false alarm—but be it as it may, I shall (and I hope without temerity) continue in business until I know more of the matter, holding myself in readiness to march at a moment's warning, and exerting every particle of military vigilance, that is dead or alive, with my escort."

Was this mere bravado? Posturing in front of the mirror of his camp journal? Most unlikely, because he was true to his word. He was always prepared to retreat at the advice of his military escort, but not one moment before it was necessary. In fact, Sargent would stay on the job quite a few moments *after* the necessary time of retreat. When the messenger reported to Hamtramck on Sargent's skepticism, Hamtramck, who was busy directing the fortification of the surveyor's camp at the mouth of Beaver Creek, sent a personal message to Sargent assuring him of the veracity of the earlier report. When it reached Sargent on the morning of September 23, New Hampshire's geographer was only half a mile from completing his range line. So he told the messenger that he would pack up and head immediately for the camp. Then he watched the messenger go back until he was out of sight and went right back to his work. As soon as he finished the last half mile, he stopped to fix a post to mark the end point and recorded bearings on several landmarks to locate it on the plats. But Sargent still was not done. Taking a bag of peach pits he had brought with him from New England, Sargent took his time walking back north up the fifth range line he had just completed, planting a peach tree every seven paces.

Just think of what that act says about the kind of people who took on this job of measuring the first American lands beyond the original thirteen. They knew that they were planting something they may not live to see; they were doing it for posterity. They were doing it for us. To be sure, there must have been some on that expedition for whom this was just another job, and those were the ones who did not have to be asked twice to retreat at the first rumor of Indian hostility. And certainly even Sargent had his share of selfish motives behind the patriotic ones that drove him to carve a new state's boundaries: he was eyeing the bounty of Ohio for himself and the land company he represented. But he was also thinking of posterity enjoying fresh peaches. In his diary that night, he wished for his little impromptu orchard "maturity in due season for the pleasure of every honest man passing this way."

While Sargent was taking his time returning to camp, Hamtramck's men were busy directing the axe men who had returned with the other surveyors. Instead of felling trees for the sightlines, or "vistas," this time they dropped as many as they could in the area around the camp, and the soldiers (with, no doubt, the aid of the horses Hamtramck had requisitioned) hauled them to the bivouac, where they became the "redoubts," or walled fortification—the predecessor of Fort Steuben, only seventeen miles farther north. In fact, Hamtramck's hastily built and temporary fortification has led to a long-standing misunderstanding of how early Hamtramck began construction of Fort Steuben.

The misunderstanding came from a chance visit on September 22, just after the redoubts were completed at the camp. Paymaster Ekuries Beatty arrived on his monthly errand, bringing the soldiers' pay, and recorded in his journal staying at the fortified camp. "Stopped at a small blockhouse today," he wrote, "on the Indian shore which Major Hamtramck had built for the security of his provisions. Saw here Capt. [John] Mills, the commissary, and Mr. Hoops, a surveyor, who told us that they expected the troops and all the surveyors in, on account of an alarm that they had received from the Indian towns." The fact that Hamtramck now needed a commissary (in Hamtramck's papers the word "commissary" always referred to the officer, not the building; the building was "the Commissary's Store") indicates that the long-awaited supplies had arrived—including the horses, the twenty head of cattle and three tons of flour. But the blockhouse that held this flour was for more than a century—because of Beatty's

Major Ekuries Beatty, whose papers preserved the 1787 Frothingham sketch of Fort Steuben. Proceedings of the Archaeological and Historical Society of Ohio, *1898.*

journal entry—mistaken for the first Fort Steuben blockhouse. Caldwell, reading Beatty's journal in 1880, reported this entry as the first reference to Fort Steuben. But Hamtramck's letter to Harmar of the previous day (September 21) makes clear that the blockhouse was at the confluence of Beaver Creek and the Ohio.

It was not long, however, before Captain Hamtramck would need to put his drills into practice and move 150 soldiers, cattle, horses and equipment to safer ground. He finished a second redoubt on September 25, and all of the farmers on the Virginia side, all up and down the Ohio, were also building pickets to protect their homes. Hamtramck could extend the fortifications he had built and connect them with a palisade of timber, but if the surveyors were to continue their work—and Hutchins urged them to do so, with Hamtramck promising military protection—the range lines and township subdivisions were being run so far south that the original camp was daily growing farther and farther from the surveyors.

Hamtramck re-fortified the detachments covering the surveyors and marched the remaining soldiers downriver to Mingo Bottom on October 4, in nearly constant rain. The surveyors were to rendezvous there in preparation for returning to their range work. The soldiers set up their tents in the rain, which continued all the following day and into the night. Lieutenant Russell Bissell arrived and reported seeing the tracks of army horses mixed with moccasin prints. A few weeks earlier, Ebenezer Sproat had sent a soldier from the line with one of the packhorses, and neither he nor the horse had been seen since. Lieutenant William Peters had also lost his horse while directing his detachment in the woods. Two hunters he sent to look for it also saw signs of Indians mixed with the hoof prints.

Sproat would become one of the most colorful figures in Ohio history and may, if the legends are accurate, be the source of Ohio's nickname, "the Buckeye State." Sproat was an imposing figure, over six feet tall at a time when the average height of the American male was five and a half feet. The Lenape who saw him called him "Hetuck," or "Big Buckeye." The name stuck. When Sproat became high sheriff of Marietta, the first capital of the state, the men of the town were called "Buckeye Men," and the term was generalized to all Ohioans. Is that really how the name arose? There are other explanations—that the Ohio chestnut or buckeye (*Aesculus glabra*) was the first tree felled when the first legal settlement was made in Marietta in 1788—but the surveyors of the Seven Ranges would prefer the Sproat version. Long before Ohio State's mascot, Brutus Buckeye, Sproat was Hetuck, the Big Buckeye.

THE ORIGINAL FORT: 1786-1787

BUILDING THE FORT

On October 11, Hamtramck marched his men north from Mingo to seek a defensible place—as Hutchins put it, "a central position somewhere between the surveyors and the south limits of their respective Ranges." After two weeks of scouting up and down the twenty-mile stretch between Mingo Bottom and the point of origin at Beaver, Hamtramck settled on a location only two and a half miles above Mingo. It was the place where the Boley, Waddle and Castleman families had been squatting a year ago and again that spring. Hamtramck described the spot to Harmar as a "Bottom about 50 or 60 yeards"—there's that French spelling again—"from the River and perfectly out [of] danger from an inundation."

The features Hamtramck was talking about can be seen by any visitor to the modern Fort Steuben. Standing at the front gate, the sally port where the guard tower faces the river, we look down on a lower plateau parallel to the river—today Route 7 runs along it. Below that is the river. The fort is on a higher shelf—safe, as Hamtramck noted, from flooding. A decade after the fort was built, the surveyor who laid out Steubenville called that second shelf "High Street." In mid-October 1786, that second shelf was the best vantage point for looking up and down the Ohio; a few months later, when the soldiers built a guard tower there, it was even better.

The five straight days of rain that had met Hamtramck's march downriver reminded him that the year was fleeting, and the temperature began to drop. Directing the axe men to begin felling trees, Hamtramck took one of the company's boats across the Ohio to the Virginia side. This had been a

Quartermaster's store (left), blockhouse and officers' quarters (right) looking southeast from the opposite blockhouse.

normal part of every bivouac along the Ohio; relations with the Virginia farmers were crucial to any frontier outpost. But this time, the object of Hamtramck's visit was different. When Hutchins visited the Virginia side, he was usually after milk, butter or other supplies he could get more easily from farmers than from his contractor, Britt. But this time, Hamtramck came back with rocks.

Even on the Virginia side, much land this far west had only been cleared for the plow for one generation. After trees were cleared and the stumps laboriously pulled by horse or oxen, the first plowing unearthed the plowman's enemy: fieldstone. Even after decades of plowing, some fields still threw up new stones at plowing, and the borders of most fields were marked by stacks or cairns of fieldstone. The hearths and chimneys of most settlers' cabins had begun their lives deep in the untilled soil of the settlers' fields. But after those chimneys were built, the farmer did not have much of a market for this unusual crop.

Captain Hamtramck already had a good relationship with one of the wealthiest farmers on the upper Ohio, the local magistrate William McMahon. McMahon had already given the soldiers and surveyors a great deal of help, and it is likely that he donated this plentiful byproduct of his more lucrative crops. At any rate, Hamtramck returned to his camp with a boatful of rocks. When the time came to build the chimneys, the other officers would appreciate Hamtramck's forethought.

When the September incidents of attacks on settlers were not followed by more concerted raids, Captain Hamtramck's main concern shifted from the

Shawnee to the advent of winter. To some extent, the two were connected, for even during the war counsels in the Shawnee villages, according to George Brickell's September 13 deposition, the warriors, like the American settlers, were also farmers who wanted to "get their Corn secured" for the winter before going to war. The soldiers' need for shelter was particularly acute, since, despite the promises of Turnbull, Marmie and Company to supply uniforms as well as food, nearly a third of the men were now without shoes.

One way the men kept warm was with hard work, more physical labor than they had seen on the geographer's line. There they had been forbidden by Hamtramck's written orders to do the work of axe men; that's what the government hired axe men for. But the axe work needed to build a fort fell under the category of military duty. An inventory of the tools at Fort Steuben does not survive, but Captain Heart's list of the tools that built Fort Harmar in the same period must have been similar. It lists two broad axes, twenty falling axes and ten fascine hatchets. Fascines were bundles of brushwood used (by the military, at least) to shore up ditches or ramparts around fortifications. The fascine hatchets cut such brush from bushes— or, as Hamtramck's men now proceeded to do, from the branches of felled trees. For trees to become logs, they needed to be stripped of branches, and the fascine hatchets were perfect for that job.

On October 27, 1786, the construction of Fort Steuben officially began. It is likely that the soldiers had already built a blockhouse to protect the supplies they had brought as soon as Hamtramck had selected the site. There is no reference to any buildings before October 27, but Hamtramck describes each company building a blockhouse and then "the other two," presumably the two officers' quarters. Yet there were four blockhouses in the completed fort. The first one, then, must have been up shortly after Hamtramck mustered in the rain at Mingo October 11.

At any rate, on that Friday, October 27, the mathematics of the blockhouses was temptingly simple. Hamtramck had three blockhouses left to build and three companies. The commander suggested a blockhouse-building contest, each company to build its own barracks. Hamtramck wrote Colonel Harmar that he had "promised as a reward six gallons of liquor to the first house Completed," and by "completed" he had a specific definition: "the up and under floors on and the chimneys build" (French spelling again). Hamtramck was thinking of his own forethought in securing chimney material. The second company to finish would get four gallons and the third, the losers, only two—plus they would have to dig the ditch for the pickets, the upright logs that linked the blockhouses in an outer defensive

Fort Steuben's master carpenter Andy Celestin uses eighteenth-century tools to create furnishings for the fort at the 2007 Fort Steuben Festival.

wall. Hamtramck confided in his commandant that the threat of digging the ditch was only a pretense to inspire competition.

In two and a half days, that is, about midday October 30, three blockhouses were ready for their roofs and chimneys. But the contest had to be suspended while all three companies constructed the officers' barracks, which took another two and a half days, until nightfall on Wednesday, November 1. On November 2, they began (or, as Hamtramck put it, "beguned") their roofs, floors and chimneys, so that by the night of November 2, the men moved into what would be their home for the next seven months.

So who won the contest? Captain Hamtramck's company, of course, because he had already assembled the rocks for his chimney. The other companies were hindered in crossing the Ohio as Hamtramck had, because, already in the first days of November, the river had frozen over—an index of how sorely needed the shelter of this yet-unnamed fort was. "The forwardness of my company on this Occasion," Hamtramck told Harmar, "can only be attributed to their great attachment to wesky." This time Hamtramck's idiosyncratic spelling probably matched the local pronunciation. The earliest settlers of western Pennsylvania and Virginia along the Ohio were largely Scots-Irish, and their generic term for distilled liquor—including the corn distillate most farmers produced there—was influenced by the Irish word for it, *usquebaugh*, which came out "whusky" or "wesky" in the earliest Ohio Valley dialect. So Hamtramck's spelling was phonetically accurate.

Particularly praised in Hamtramck's account was the work of a young lieutenant, William Kersey, who had taken over Mercer's company, apparently due to disciplinary issues that impeded Hamtramck's command during the Indian scare. Both of the other two captains in Hamtramck's command, William McCurdy and John Mercer, were guilty of insubordination, a surprisingly unmilitary failing for two officers who had served with distinction in the Revolution. But it was a sign of the precarious status of the first federal army. As we have seen, the new army had only been approved the previous April and was a tentative experiment. Many Americans felt that, with the Revolution over, the United States had no further need for an army. Also, since the new nation was still operating under the Articles of Confederation—the Constitutional Convention would not meet until the following spring, and the first presidential election was more than two years away—promotions in rank depended on the states, since technically the "federal" army was a loose conglomeration of troops recruited by each state.

The resulting confusion created a disciplinary problem for Hamtramck, whether or not it was the cause of the insubordination. When Hamtramck had been given command of the three companies, Harmar and Secretary of War Henry Knox had wanted to establish him as a major. But Hamtramck had been recruited by New York, and New York had a full complement of majors. Major Nicholas Fish was due to retire his commission, but both Captain Hamtramck and Captain Doughty were in line for the promotion. Knox wrote to Harmar on September 26, 1786, that he would like to see both men as majors, but he had to petition Congress. Doughty offered a glorious solution: he would be happy to let Hamtramck be a major ahead of him if Doughty could receive a major's pay.

Until the matter was resolved, however, the chain of command in the three companies labored under the intolerable imbalance of a captain commanding two other captains. This could not have sat well with McCurdy and Mercer. The specific insubordination by McCurdy was essentially abandoning his detachment at the height of the Indian scare on September 19. The charge was AWOL. On September 22, Hamtramck issued the following arrest order to McCurdy:

Sir

You are ordered in arrest for having without leave absented your self from your Column when on March on the 19th Instant. For neglect of Duty on the 20th in not fixing the advanced guard and out flanks agreeably to the order of March when it was your Business so to do.—For wilfull disobedience of orders on the 21st in Making your Company File their arms Contrary to my positive orders, and disrespect contrary to Military Subordination good order, and discipline.

JFHamtramck

Cmndt of the 1s Regt.

Mercer's offense was many times more horrible than a mere AWOL charge. If it happened today, it might become known as "Trousergate." Captain Mercer's crime? Distributing woolen britches to his soldiers without authorization.

It's easy to paint Hamtramck either as a mean old miser or a by-the-book military nerd, but there was an important principle behind the captain's

The guardhouse under construction, November 2009. The lower-level space on the right was the "black hole" for keeping prisoners; on the left was storage.

strict adherence to the letter of military law here, beyond the admittedly important principle of military discipline. After all, you can't have your officers deciding which orders they will obey and which they can ignore. The principle was that, because the future of the army was uncertain, Harmar could not be sure that Congress would approve funds for further uniforms as these wore out. Hamtramck could not release the clothing from military stores without written approval from Harmar. Hamtramck even wrote to Harmar on October 21 for permission to give the coats of dead and deserted soldiers to other soldiers who had none. When Mercer ignored protocol, he needed to be disciplined.

So it was that the construction of one of the blockhouses was directed by Lieutenant William Kersey. Over the next few weeks, the various detachments came one by one to the new fort as their surveyors left for the season. There was still a great deal of paperwork to be done—the "platting," or recording of the range and township lines on maps—but a few surveyors could do that over the winter based on the surveyors' field notes. Hutchins and Matthews wintered in comfort at Justice McMahon's. But Sargent left for Pittsburgh on November 15, and Tupper returned to New England the same day. One by one, the other surveyors went home, and their escorts swelled the barracks at the fort. On December 2, Hutchins sent the full report (most importantly the expenses) to Congress. The total charge to Congress for surveying Seven Ranges came to $9,741, itemized as follows:

Geographer's Salary (Hutchins) at $6.00 a day: $4044.00
Deputies' expenses, 1785: 1673.62
Deputies' pay at $2.00 per mile, 604 miles: 1208.36
Message to Delawares and Wyandotts: 94.85
Travel Expenses to Philadelphia: 115.46
Canoe: 10.00
Tin can for reports: 1.00
Deputies' expenses, 1786: 2379.11

Cold and snow hampered building, but much of December was spent in finishing the fort. The living quarters were finished but vulnerable without a picket (or "piquet" in Hamtramck's spelling, which was actually quite common in eighteenth-century American writing). The soldiers dug trenches wide enough to accommodate upright logs and built a log wall connecting all four blockhouses and the two officers' quarters. The outer walls of all six buildings would form part of the outer defense. Log

Reenactors face inspection at the Ohio Valley Frontier Days, June 2008.

palisades were also erected from the main gate down to the river so that soldiers or supplies landing or departing could be protected right to their embarkation point.

Before the pickets could be finished, however, there were several more smaller buildings to go inside the compound. Two that would—like the barracks—form part of the outer wall were the commissary, for the storage of all food supplies, and the quartermaster's store, for the storage of all non-food supplies (tools, weapons and, of course, the infamous woolen britches). Two additional structures would be offset from the outer wall in case of fire or explosion: the artificer's (blacksmith's) shop and the magazine, where the gunpowder was stored. By the time all of these buildings, and the picket wall, were up, December was over—and so was 1786.

The day after New Year's 1787, Hamtramck reported the fortifications complete except for the pickets. He also replied to Harmar's dispatch of December 21, in which the colonel had given Hamtramck the honor of naming the new fort. The previous federal fort, Harmar's headquarters at the mouth of the Muskingum, had been named for Harmar himself, and he suggested that Hamtramck follow suit, naming the new installation Fort Hamtramck. The captain had other ideas. "I am Exceedingly obliged to you," Hamtramck replied, "for the Compliment you have been pleased to pass on me in the naming of our Fort, and must beg to be Excused from such an honor. Since you have Directed me to inform you what name I would like to call it, I would propose to name it <u>Fort Stuben</u> and your approbation to it will infinitely oblige me." And so the world's first reference to Fort Steuben was a misspelling. That particular spelling was, however, quite common: many Revolution-era documents identify the inspector general in a French form he seemed to enjoy: "Baron de Stuben."

Near the end of January, Geographer Hutchins spent his last few days on the job at Fort Steuben before departing for New York on January 27 to report to Congress. All seven range lines were finished, but the area within the range lines was to be subdivided into townships six miles square (with the townships near the river, of course, in irregular shapes). Only the first four ranges, and seven townships in range five, were so subdivided. Under the circumstances, Hutchins thought that a good season's work. Congress did not share the geographer's opinion.

DAILY LIFE AT FORT STEUBEN

With his three companies finally falling into garrison life after months in the woods, camp commander Jean Francois Hamtramck—major as far as the brass was concerned, though captain under the Articles of Confederation—conducted a thorough, top-to-bottom inspection on January 27 to assess the personnel and equipment of Fort Steuben. The return for Captain McCurdy's company was not included in Hamtramck's report—McCurdy was still in confinement at Fort McIntosh pending a ruling on his insubordination charge—and even after his reinstatement, Hamtramck lamented that McCurdy's books were "not regularly kept." But the two returns that do survive, one for Mercer's company and one for Hamtramck's, give us a fairly detailed picture of the garrison at Fort Steuben. Each company had a full complement of one captain, a lieutenant, an ensign, four sergeants, four corporals, one drummer and one fifer and forty-three privates, not counting one in the infirmary and one "on command." The forty-five privates thus accounted for was fifteen short of regulation. Hamtramck's company was similarly situated: all forty-five privates were on duty, but he was short one lieutenant and one corporal. In Mercer's company, one sergeant and two

Captain (or Major) Hamtramck's daily reports issued from this desk in what was the only private room at Fort Steuben.

privates were listed as deserted, and in Hamtramck's one private was listed as "taken prisoner" and another dead.

The private reported dead was, or so Hamtramck assumed, the man Ebenezer Sproat had sent on an errand with his horse on September 19, never to be seen again by the surveyors. On October 4, Lieutenant Russell Bissel had returned from rescuing another missing soldier from the woods, and on the way back he found the tracks of Sproat's horse with moccasin prints alongside them. Three weeks later, on October 26, Hamtramck reported that a Virginia hunter had found the body of a soldier "kill^d and scalp^d." Hamtramck promised Harmar that he would investigate, but no further word on Fort Steuben's only casualty appears in Hamtramck's papers—not even the soldier's name.

The foodstuffs on hand at Fort Steuben were also tabulated. Captain John Mills had transferred to an artillery unit on January 15, so his assistant, Lieutenant William Peters, took over as commissary. More important, in light of Mercer's premature allotment of woolen britches, was the inspection of the quartermaster's provisions. Quartermaster Ensign Francis Luse showed for each company fifty-five hats, coats, vests, "bretches," gloves and stockings in use. There were no shoes on hand, though there were fifteen shoe buckles. Mercer's company showed 52 muskets in use, and Hamtramck's 53. Assuming a similar number in the third company, there were over 150 flintlocks at Fort Steuben. For Mercer's 52 muskets there were 624 cartridges in the cartridge boxes each soldier carried—an even dozen per musket—and 815 more ready-made in the quartermaster's store. For Hamtramck's 53 muskets there were 636 cartridges at hand—again, a dozen apiece—and 870 in storage. Mercer's men had fired 43 times in January and Hamtramck's men 25. Some of those would have been in drills and target practice and some for signaling. Both Hutchins and Hamtramck report men who were lost in the woods firing shots to signal their location.

When Hutchins left to report to Congress, he assumed that it would be April or May before surveyors could get back into the ranges. But the urgent need to sell the land could not wait for spring. Although all the state geographers had left the Ohio, three trained surveyors who had helped them remained at Fort Steuben: John Matthews, Charles Smith and Israel Ludlow. A warm February brought two thaws: the first on the range lines and the second in Hamtramck's attitude toward McCurdy. Actually, Hamtramck had indicated to Harmar as early as December 15 that he was willing to release McCurdy and not pursue a court-martial if McCurdy were to "acknowledge the charges and himself make application to me." Two months later, McCurdy sent this note, which, though brief, met Hamtramck's criteria: "With Respect to the charges of the 19th and 20th of September you have Exhibited against me I assure you that I had no intention to Disobey your Orders, and as for the one of 21st I Declare to you on my honor I did not mean to treat you with Disrespect." That was enough for Hamtramck; he released McCurdy and allowed the captain to resume command of his company. A new captain, David Strong, was transferred to Fort Steuben to replace Mercer.

There were other changes in personnel. On February 4, Hamtramck summoned John Matthews to the fort. Hutchins and Martin had praised his abilities in keeping the supplies in order at the surveyors' camp, and Hamtramck thought he would make a good commissary. After a few days' training with Lieutenant Peters (who had himself only held the position for about a month), Matthews took over on February 8. A week later, Thursday, February 15, Israel Ludlow went into the woods to resume the township lines on the fifth range. As in the fall, Hamtramck supplied him with a military escort and a packhorse loaded with corn. A few days later, Charles

Stripped view of the rope beds used by soldiers at Fort Steuben. With a canvas mattress filled with straw and a wool blanket, these beds are more comfortable than they look.

Smith would also head out with another detachment—and horse, which Hamtramck, remembering the horses lost, as he supposed, to the Indians, lamented. "More expense than good," he complained to Harmar, "for I am sure the Indians, being out trapping, will steal the horses." Before the Revolution, Hamtramck had himself been a fur trader with the French Canadians in this territory, and he knew the seasons.

While the surveyors were going out into the woods, so were a few of Mercer's soldiers—without permission. On February 16, Hamtramck sent out eight search parties after deserters, with no success. Hamtramck spent most of March at Fort Pitt conferring with other officers about how best to deploy troops as the surveyors moved down the river. The chief officer of Fort Steuben was beginning to see that his first command was not destined to be a permanent garrison.

To the First American Regiment, the advent of April always meant raids on squatters. In 1785, it had been Captain Armstrong; in 1786, it had been Hamtramck himself. This time, an ensign with a German accent as thick as Hamtramck's Belgian French one would have the honors: Cornelius Ryker Seydam. Armstrong and Hamtramck had left fairly detailed lists of the people they displaced. This time, half of the families had fled by the time Seydam's detachment arrived on April 4, so only six of the twelve family names are preserved: Lamartine, Mariel, Ross, Welsh, Delaney and McCleans.

On April 7, Hamtramck was ordered to take over the command of Fort Harmar while the colonel was conferring with Congress. This time, there was to be no question of Hamtramck's authority with the captains:

he was finally promoted to major. At Fort Steuben, his company would be commanded by James Bradford, who was also summarily promoted in the process, from lieutenant to captain.

With the arrival of spring, the state geographers began to return to the Ohio Valley, reporting in at Fort Steuben. Absalom Martin, who had never left the valley and had been staying at Wheeling with Ebenezer Zane's family, was ready to continue surveying. He had lingered at the Zane house longer than Hutchins, who had to leave in January to report to Congress, and Matthews, who had preceded him onto the line. What kept Martin back at Zane's was not so much the Virginia cuisine, which was enticing enough in itself, or the equally plentiful tales of the "Battle of Fort Henry," of which Zane's sister Elizabeth was the heroine. Almost a full year after the British surrender at Yorktown, Americans on the frontier were still being harried by the Indian allies of the British, sometimes with British help. On September 11, 1782, Betty, Isaac and Ebenezer Zane were huddled in Fort Henry while Shawnee and Lenape warriors kept up a siege. The Virginians kept them off with their Kentucky rifles, but they were getting low on powder. Betty knew where her father (or, in some accounts, her brother) had buried a keg of black powder, and she reasoned that the Indians would not fire on a woman. She was right. The Indians allowed her access to her cabin. She knew that if they saw her carrying a keg of powder, they might try to stop her. So she filled her apron with powder and ran back to the fort, saving the day.

Still, it was not the prospect of conversation with the renowned Betty Zane that kept Martin in the Ohio Valley. It was Betty's seventeen-year-old niece, Catherine. Two years later, after surveying Marietta farther downriver,

Typical view in the officers' barracks (off duty).

Martin would marry Catherine and apply for the first ferry license in the territory. The town he founded is still called Martins Ferry. But on April 10, 1787, Martin went back into the woods to continue laying out the townships. Ludlow left the same day and Smith on April 17. James Simpson, who came back from Maryland a few days later, joined them on the Seven Ranges the following week, April 24. So hopeful were the surveyors of a productive spring that geographer Benjamin Tupper, with his son Anselm, also a trained surveyor, even began running an eighth range. The next day, however, word of an Indian attack killing three men came to the surveyors. They dropped their work and fled to Wheeling, with Smith, Martin and Ludlow arriving on May 5. For three days there was no sign of Charles Smith. On May 8, the three surveyors rode to Fort Steuben, hoping Smith had made it to safety there. He was not there when they arrived but finally came in two days later, on May 10.

Ensign Adams led a detachment out of Fort Steuben for one final raid on Ohio squatters, destroying twelve more homes. This time, none of the names was recorded; we don't even know Ensign Adams's first name. On May 11, a second Indian attack closer to Fort Steuben—near what would be modern Yorkville, Ohio—killed one man and two children. The surveyors decided to stay at the fort. A week later, May 19, Major Hamtramck returned to his first command with the paymaster, Major Beatty—a bit wistfully, perhaps, knowing that the new fort's days were numbered. On May 23, the major sent his commissary, John Matthews, across the river to requisition packhorses for a move downriver. Fort Harmar would be their new home as they continued to survey the Ohio Territory. When Matthews returned on May 25, there had been more shuffling of personnel; the three companies were now under the command of Captain John Smith, Captain David Strong and Captain William Mercer. Strong moved his company out of Fort Steuben on May 26, Smith and Mercer on May 30. The commissary, John Matthews, was left alone with the supplies.

But not for long. Having turned all the packhorses over to the companies, Matthews was left to load the supplies onto a sail-powered keelboat for storage in Wheeling. He left before noon, but the winds were so strong against him that he had to stop at 2:00 p.m. until they subsided or risk losing the supplies. When he reached Wheeling the following day, his duties as the third and last commissary of Fort Steuben were over. In fact, the fort itself was history. But Matthews would visit Fort Steuben one more time. A civilian, despite working for Hamtramck, Matthews remained at work on the plats at the home of Justice McMahon at Beech Bottom, ten miles below the fort on the

The enlisted men's barracks in the blockhouses had a double fireplace in the center, warming both sides of a divided barracks.

Virginia side. Despite the scalping of a trespasser on the Ohio side on July 31, Matthews decided to risk a similar fate, lured by the prices that ginseng, which grew wild around Fort Steuben, was fetching in the East. Crossing the Ohio on September 20 with a few Virginia friends, he spent more than a week digging the root all through the ranges he had helped survey. Little did he know that other Indian attacks occurred throughout the area during his absence, and only in retrospect could he tell his diary how narrowly he had missed being captured himself:

> *We were much surprised to hear that three men had been killed and one taken prisoner by the Indians, about ten miles up Cross Creek, who were out after ginseng on Sunday last. Two of the party made their escape. They had also killed a family the week following, up Wheeling Creek, and done considerable other damage. While we were out we were very careless and came on their trail, but fortunately, they did not fall in with us. I feel very happy that I have reached my old quarters, and will give them liberty to take my scalp if they catch me after ginseng again this year.*

On the morning of the second day of Matthews's ginseng expedition, 350 miles east of Fort Steuben in New York City, the largest land sale in the history of the world began. Fort Steuben had helped make it possible, but after only seven months of service, Fort Steuben was being retired. A million and a half acres were up for sale, but when the sale ended on October 9, only 108,431 had been sold—and of that "sale," nearly 10 percent, some 10,000 acres, were not paid for. The federal treasury actually saw only $117,108 from the sale—or $107,000 after subtracting the cost of the survey. The national debt at the time was $75 million.

That was not the only disappointment. The dream of underpaid veterans of the Revolution getting their long overdue reward did not materialize. Oh, the land was cheap enough, at a dollar an acre—even in 1787 that was a real bargain. But the rules of the sale stipulated that purchasers could not buy parcels smaller than a square mile, or 640 acres. To buy the smallest parcel would take five months' salary for a U.S. congressman ($1,500 a year). No wonder most of the land in the Seven Ranges remained unsold for a long time. The very land where Fort Steuben sat was not sold for another decade, and by then the fort was gone. It would stay gone—for about two hundred years.

REBUILDING FORT STEUBEN

EARLY ATTEMPTS

What happened to Fort Steuben after the last soldier left on that final day of May 1787? No one really knows. The last reference to its existence is no later than the following fall. On October 12, 1787, Virginia magistrate William McMahon, whose farm had been home to the Fort Steuben surveyors the previous winter, received news of an elderly man attacked and killed near the abandoned fort. He sent a party to investigate; they recovered the body outside of the fort—and that was the last datable reference to the original fort.

Ten years later, in 1797, when Bazaleel Wells began surveying the boundaries of a town to be called Steubenville after the fort, there was no indication of any preexisting structure, and Wells ran what he called "High Street" right over the site. As the town (and later the city) began to grow, the residents knew about the old fort, but they were too busy starting a new community to worry about its whereabouts. In 1825, the son of the regimental paymaster of the frontier, Reverend Charles C. Beatty, moved to Steubenville, and when he heard talk about the fort, he realized that he had some of the original references to it among his father's papers. In 1850, he came across a sketch of the fort and on September 14 told the Steubenville newspapers what history he had reconstructed. He loaned his father's journal to the *Magazine of American History*, which printed it in 1877. But he held back the sketch of the fort, which did not appear in the magazine.

A few years later, when J.A. Caldwell printed his massive *History of Belmont and Jefferson Counties, Ohio* (Wheeling, 1880), the account of Fort

A soldier's pastimes—a twist of tobacco, a tavern pipe, cards, dice, a jaw harp—filled the long winter between the halt in the surveying in October and the resumption in April.

Steuben there reminded Beatty of his father's sketch, and he loaned it to the *Steubenville Herald*, which published a rotogravure copy on December 6, 1881. In the accompanying article, Beatty recorded his father's assertion that the sketch was not made by him but by Lieutenant Ebenezer Frothingham, who was killed in the Indian attack known as "Harmar's Defeat" on October 22, 1790.

Caldwell's account included, for the first time in any recorded story of Fort Steuben, an ending to the story. In Caldwell's version, the fort was totally destroyed by fire in 1790. There are several difficulties with that story, however. First, it is odd that there is no reference to a fire until ninety years after it supposedly took place. Second, there is no discernible physical evidence of such a fire. When the archaeology of the site began in the 1980s, no one on the archaeological team believed the story of the fire. However, the chief investigator, Professor Jack Boyde of Franciscan University of Steubenville, offered a rival theory.

Boyde pointed out that when the closing of Fort McIntosh was imminent, about the same time as the demise of Fort Steuben, the last remaining officer wrote to Colonel Harmar begging for him to authorize a detachment of even a few men to protect the structure—not from the Indians but from the streams of American immigrants floating down the Ohio to Kentucky homesteads, taking timbers from the abandoned fort. The most likely fate of Fort Steuben is that some of the earliest American dwellings in southern Ohio, Kentucky and Indiana were pieces of the fort. Precut lumber lie unprotected sixty yards (or "yeards," as Hamtramck spelled it) from the

Rebuilding Fort Steuben

Curator Bill Croskey (left) shows George Washington impersonator Bryan Cunning (right) the first federal land office at the 2007 Fort Steuben Festival.

Ohio. The river was downhill from the fort. And wood floats. What could be simpler?

Whatever the fate of the original fort, it stayed in the imagination of the people of Steubenville once the Reverend Beatty shared his father's papers in 1850. In the decades after that, it caught the imagination of a new group of immigrants to Steubenville. Immediately after the American Civil War, a wave of German immigrants came to most Midwestern U.S. cities, and Steubenville was no exception. Since the number one point of connection Germans felt for the United States was the Prussian general Baron von Steuben, German-Americans were delighted to find a city on the Ohio bearing his name. By the 1870s, there were enough German-Americans in Steubenville to warrant a German-language newspaper, the *Steubenville Germania*, founded in 1876. R. Schnorrenberg, the founder and editor, ran a series of articles about the fort, resulting in the city's German societies marking 1886 as the centennial of the fort's construction, which they celebrated by raising a garrison flag at what they supposed was the site of the fort, then the residence of Judge John H. Miller on the corner of High and Adams Streets.

The Caldwell myth of the fort burning down in 1790 gained significance as the centennial of that supposed event drew near, and Schnorrenberg decided that Steubenville should celebrate the anniversary—rejoicing not in the idea of the fire but in the fort and its connection with von Steuben. Schnorrenberg's name for the celebration was brilliant, a dual-language pun. He decided to call it *Steubenfeier*, which means "Steuben

Celebration"—but the German word *feier*, "celebration," sounds just like a two-syllable pronunciation of the English word *fire*. The *Feier* would be the centennial of the *fire*. The celebration was to be more than just a party, however. Having pulled up their roots in Germany, these new Americans, seeking new roots here, tried to identify the location of Fort Steuben and even contemplated the first of many attempts at reconstructing it. The *Feier* was held Monday, August 25. The *Daily Herald* described the festivities:

> *Monday opened with sunshine, waving banners, the music of bands, and gathering crowds to celebrate the memory of Baron Steuben, the Prussian soldier who aided the American cause so nobly in the revolutionary war. It also commemorates the destruction of Fort Steuben, which the Government had erected on the site of the present city of Steubenville, for the protection of the surveyors who were already at work preparing the territory northwest of the Ohio for settlement. A sketch of this fort and the man after whom it was named appropriately precedes an account of the celebration itself.*

The celebration became something of a trial run for the city's own centennial seven years later. Zeal for the celebration led to a desire to rebuild Fort Steuben, and at the March 29, 1897 meeting of the Centennial Committee in the City Council Chambers, Steubenville realtor and insurance agent Josiah C. Ault introduced a plan to do so. "Before being called to order," the *Daily Herald* story of April 2 read, "the project of reproducing Fort Steuben was discussed, and it is possible now that it will be rebuilt along lines suggested by J.C. Ault who said it could be rebuilt very reasonably using slabs, and he is to see several sawmill owners about the slabs."

There was only one problem with Ault's plan. While Judge Miller, then retired, was more than happy to have a commemorative flag placed on his estate, he was unlikely to want to demolish his stately brick home, one of the first grand homes in Steubenville, built before 1800. When the judge died in 1891, his son Edward and daughter, Mrs. Elizabeth Pratt, inherited the estate, and they had no interest in turning their father's home into a log fort. When Mrs. Pratt, the last heir, died, the property was sold—ironically, in the year of another centennial, the 100th anniversary of the incorporation of Steubenville as a town (1905). High and Adams was now prime downtown real estate. The new owner, Horace Simmons, had converted the block into five building lots, though he announced that the old mansion would stay. "Site of Fort Steuben Is to Be Built Up" read the front page of the *Herald* on February 17, 1905. "Historic Old Spot Will Be Turned Into Building Lots."

A rustic woodcarver's bench used to make shingles for Fort Steuben's roof. The forked log held a slab of wood, and a draw knife shaved it at one end for overlapping.

But the business leaders who moved into the lots were not without historical conscience. On Wednesday, July 23, 1913, the city planted a granite marker with a brass plate designating the presumed location of the corners of Fort Steuben and held a public dedication the following day. Some historical articles have wrongly dated the granite posts at 1886, confusing them with the substantial marker flags placed by the German societies for the fort's centennial. For more than six decades, the markers were the only reminder of Fort Steuben ever having been there, and like most urban areas that grew up around a fort, it looked like reclaiming the spot would never be a possibility. History, like the Ohio River, flows in one direction only.

THE ARCHAEOLOGY OF FORT STEUBEN

In the face of such pessimism, in the late 1970s, the chair of the history department at the University of Steubenville, Professor Jack Boyde, obtained permission to conduct an archaeological field school on the site, some of which was now overgrown with weeds and even bushes. In the summer of 1979, Professor Boyde's first archaeology students began digging near the

Professor Phil Fitzgibbons (right) directs the Franciscan University of Steubenville Archaeological Field School at the Fort Steuben dig.

granite markers to see if they could discover signs of the fort. Since the closest university with an archaeology program (that is, until Boyde later started his own at the University of Steubenville, which by then had added "Franciscan" to its name) was the University of Pittsburgh, Boyde found a young research assistant named Phil Fitzgibbons who was eager to help lead the excavation.

That first summer, the excavation did not reach deep enough to find artifacts of the fort era, and the following year there was no further work. But in 1981, a second group of Boyde's students tried again, and then again in 1983. The artifacts began more and more pointing to the fort era: clay pipe stems (which can be dated by the width of the air passage), period buttons and clay musket balls. The clay balls help suggest an eighteenth-century military site, because the army used them for target practice in order to save on lead. Also, the clay ball bursts into a cloud of fine powder on impact, making the result of a soldier's shot immediately obvious. No self-respecting frontier hunter would need such a thing.

Like any good archaeologist, Professor Boyde did not confine his research to the ground. Two of his senior students, Melinda Boyde (you guessed it: the professor's daughter) and Katie Carrigg (whose father, Dr. John Carrigg, was also a history professor at the university), were writing their senior theses on the fort, and, following Dad's lead to papers at the Library of Congress and the William L. Clements Library at the University of Michigan, the two young women found the original letters of Hamtramck, Hutchins and Harmar, which formed the basis of most of what we now know about the fort. This book quite literally could not have been written without Boyde and Carrigg's work.

If the every-second-summer pattern had continued, the fourth dig should have taken place in 1985. But by postponing it one year, Boyde and Fitzgibbons were able to have a team of lucky students conduct an excavation on the bicentennial of the fort's initial construction. Early Tuesday morning, June 24, 1986, the first trowels hit the earth at the Fort Steuben site, then owned by the Ohio Power Company, though the company had vacated that location a few years before. This time, the artifacts were more startling than ever, though not connected with the fort era. Completely unexpectedly, the team uncovered Native American artifacts dating between AD 700 and 900—the Hopewell era. With that kind of find, Boyde and Fitzgibbons could not wait another year to continue the dig, so they quickly arranged a field school for the fall semester. Beginning again September 8, they struck archaeological gold: two pottery pieces dating perhaps as early as AD 100, which would make them possibly Adena artifacts. These were not the earliest native pieces found in the area: the East Steubenville site directly across the river from Steubenville dates to 2,000 BC. But this was sufficiently exciting for college students on their first dig.

A deeper portion of the archaeological dig at the Fort Steuben site.

Ohio Power continued to be encouraging, not only to Boyde and his students but also to a growing number of Steubenville residents interested in reviving the fort. Oddly enough, Ohio Power's ownership of the site may have been an integral element in making the Fort Steuben reconstruction possible. Because the company did not need the property and could build a great deal of community goodwill by helping to preserve history, making it available to the archaeologists was a no-brainer. But could the public use of this block go beyond a summer field school?

What happened next was another extraordinary link in the extremely unlikely story of rebuilding an eighteenth-century fort in the middle of a twentieth-century urban area. When Professor Boyde was invited to give a public lecture on the excavations for the bicentennial of the fort in 1986, a pair of retired teachers, Elizabeth King and Geraldine Cohen, asked a simple question: what would it take to build a full-size replica of the fort in the exact location of the original? Years later, Boyde told me that his first reaction to the question was panic. What would it take? What it would take would be nearly impossible. It would take the corporate owner of the lot to relinquish it. By 1986, that already seemed likely. But it would take so much more. It would take a great deal of money. It would take a lot of hard work by hundreds of volunteers. And lots of money. It would take the support of public officials at every level: city, county, state and federal. And money. It would take discovering, and then deciphering, and then meeting thousands of arcane regulations. And it would take money. It would take a mountain of paperwork, a high degree of community involvement and consummate people skills. And, finally, it would take a great deal of you-know-what.

The Kings were joined by several other community leaders in their dream of rebuilding Fort Steuben. In May 1986, they first met to form a nonprofit organization, the Old Fort Steuben Project, Inc. They vowed that within five years they would start construction on the fort. This was before they even had title to the land. But negotiations in that direction would begin immediately. In November, they met with the city, which owned a 0.7-acre L-shaped lot in the block, and Ohio Power, which owned the remaining 3.15 acres. The city's assistance was not limited to the land, however. The 1986 dig, and others in the future, were funded in part by grants distributed through the city's Urban Projects authority.

The next step, and it is still ongoing, was the serious fundraising. The American Association of University Women, which can be considered the inspiration behind the Old Fort Steuben Project, received a major grant for the project in February 1987. Other donors came to a Friday morning

Tomorrow's archaeologists learn how to sift artifacts out of the soil at the Fort Steuben Summer Youth Educational Program, 2006.

breakfast press conference on November 18, 1988, where project president Elizabeth King unveiled the first architectural sketches of the first blockhouse. In the twenty-two months in between, project members did their homework. They visited as many reconstructed forts as they could find and contacted HearthStone, Inc., of Dandridge, Tennessee, a leader in log house construction, to discover the challenges (and costs) of building authentic blockhouses.

Finally, late Friday morning, June 23, 1989, project members and local and state officials picked up shovels for the groundbreaking ceremony. In addition to the project's president, Elizabeth King, Vice-president Charles Govey (then publisher of the Steubenville *Herald Star*), Treasurer Douglas Naylor and Secretary Barbara Topp, committee members who hoisted shovels included Betty Applegate, Jack Boyde, Geraldine Cohen, D.E. "Sam" Henderson, Otto Jack Jr., Richard Q. King and David Hindman, who also happened to be Steubenville's mayor at the time. Other officials included Ohio representative Jerry Krupinski and Ohio Historical Society chief curator Amos Loveday. Eight weeks later, the first blockhouse was finished. While Hearthstone engineers placed the large square logs with heavy machinery—each beam the center of a large Canadian hemlock—much of the finishing work was done by students in the senior carpentry class at the Jefferson County Joint Vocational Schools, under teachers Paul Nuzum and Russell Ensell.

The following summer, 1990, a second blockhouse was completed, and WSTV-WRKY radio donated $10,000 to connect the two completed blockhouses with pickets—more than one hundred rough-cut logs, each weighing over two hundred pounds. Hamilton Surveying of Steubenville donated its expertise to make sure the pickets and the corners of the blockhouses lined up. What could be more natural in the Fort Steuben compound than surveyors, even two hundred years after the measuring of the Seven Ranges? That September, the State of Ohio released the first of two $50,000 payments for the remaining two blockhouses—the largest single contribution yet, and the first public funds on the state level. Still, local contributions at that point totaled more than $130,000. Without those local contributions, the state (and, later, federal) moneys might not have materialized.

At a ceremony on Saturday, October 13, officially presenting the check (graced with musket drills by the First Company of the Fort McIntosh

Visitors to the 2009 Ohio Valley Frontier Days watch Fort Steuben's artificer, John Boilegh, demonstrate his craft.

Garrison reenactment group of Beaver, Pennsylvania), State Senator Robert Burch made just that point in praising the leadership of Mrs. King. "You don't have to wait for someone else to do it," he told the crowd. "You don't have to wait for the federal or state government—or any government."

The following summer, in June 1991, I first became involved in the fort reconstruction when the Fort Steuben Festival Committee—a group of business leaders unconnected with, but eager to work with, the project committee—took over Steubenville's summer "Homecoming Festival" and changed its direction, giving it a historical theme and tying it to the Fort Steuben site. In order to promote the festival, they felt they needed to promote the fort. *But how do you build an emotional attachment to a group of buildings?* asked festival chairman Attorney William Fisher. We need to put a face on Fort Steuben, he said. For better or worse, the face the committee put on it was mine; I have been wearing a wig and talking in a bad Prussian accent for Fort Steuben ever since.

Even though the Fort Steuben Festival was a separate entity from the reconstruction project for the next few years (though of course working closely with the project), the festival provided an attraction to bring people to the fort each June. With only two blockhouses and a log picket, it could be hard for visitors to imagine the whole fort. Reenactors and demonstrations of fort-era crafts helped fill out the picture each June. But while the festival committee did its thing, the Fort Steuben Project, Inc., kept going forward. With the funds from the Ohio Historical Society (secured with the help of State representative Jerry Krupinski), the third blockhouse was underway shortly after the first fort festival (June 14–16, 1991), and the fourth was constructed in April 1992. For the second Fort Steuben Festival, then, all four blockhouses were up, though the pickets still did not enclose the compound. Volunteers continued to donate time and services: not just the members of the project and the Festival Committee but also, in addition to the major players already mentioned—the City of Steubenville, Ohio Power and the Joint Vocational School—groups such as the local Carpenter's Union, Hamilton Surveying, Columbia Gas (which, in addition to donating services, sponsored a series of radio Public Service Announcements about the fort), the Steubenville Rotary (service and monetary grants), Company 4 of the 463rd Battalion Army Reserve of Weirton and the Ohio Civilian Conservation Corps.

For the third Fort Steuben Festival in 1993, no new buildings were added, but most of the pickets were up. In 1994, the first of two officers' quarters were added. Also unveiled in time for the fourth festival was a painting of how Fort Steuben would have looked in 1797 by noted historical painter Jess

Between October 1786 and May 1787, Fort Steuben had three commissaries: Captain John Mills, Lieutenant William Peters and civilian John Matthews.

Hager. Prints were available, and the painting was featured in an art show of colonial and early frontier subjects for the 1994 festival.

In 1995, the second officers' quarters appeared. In that year, the Fort Steuben Project took over the festival. Just before the sixth festival in June 1996, the project received word of being awarded an Appalachian Grant, administered through Jefferson Community College. The project applied for the amount of the total cost of the remaining buildings, $62,000, but only $25,000 was approved. Another boon that year was the Ohio Humanities Council donating the Northwest Ordinance display it had constructed for the 1987 Bicentennial of the Ordinance. This had been a traveling exhibit that had come to Steubenville in 1987, before there was a single blockhouse on the site. The donation of the display was a win-win for the Humanities Council, since it really did not have the facilities to store the now decade-old display, and yet, being a humanities group, it didn't have the heart to destroy something so beautiful. So the display found a permanent home at Fort Steuben, which was, after all, an integral part of the land development leading to the Northwest Ordinance.

Rebuilding Fort Steuben

In October 1996, construction began on the seventh and eighth buildings, the commissary and the quartermaster's store. By the beginning of Steubenville's bicentennial year, then, 1997, eight of the ten proposed buildings were complete. The energy of that bicentennial, and anticipation of the bicentennial of Ohio's statehood in 2003, urged the Fort Steuben Project into a new phase of development. Instead of just trying to raise enough money for the remaining two buildings, the project's Richard Q. King spearheaded the planning of something larger: turning what was essentially a gravel parking lot surrounding the fort into an attractive park with grass, trees and a fountain. The price tag was in the neighborhood of $1.5 million, but once again, King's strategy was to begin local fundraising immediately as a sign to the grant agencies of community support. The public moneys, however, came from a number of sources: $200,000 in state grants, $10,000 from the Steubenville Bicentennial Committee and another $10,000 from Jefferson County. These start-up funds were in place by March 1999, and initial construction of the park started right after the ninth Fort Festival, June 12–13.

In September 1999, the last two buildings of Fort Steuben were complete: the artificer's shop and the hospital. The presence of the hospital is something of a compromise between documentary and living history in the reconstruction, since the original 1787 sketches of the fort do not show a hospital or infirmary. It is likely that Dr. Elliott used the officers' quarters or one of the other buildings (perhaps the quartermaster's store) to treat the soldiers and store his medicinal supplies. But to showcase the company surgeon's role—he is mentioned, for instance, in Hamtramck's written orders to the detachments guarding the surveyors: the soldiers were required to be checked by the surgeon before they were cleared to go out to the ranges—project members felt that it would facilitate presentation to have a separate space for the doctor.

Just before Christmas 1999, the Old Fort Steuben Project received its best Christmas gift ever. Through the help of U.S. congressman Bob Ney, the fort received a $900,000 Ohio Scenic Byways Grant to complete Fort Steuben Park. Two months later, ancillary grants raised the total to $1.25 million. Key to the grant was a new twist that would enhance the status of the fort and the park in the Ohio tourism community: the park would be home to a visitors' center that would be the starting point for travelers visiting the whole length of the Ohio River—hence the "Scenic Byways" part of the title. The 462 miles of Route 7 along the river from East Liverpool to Cincinnati were declared a byway by Congress in 1998 (in fact, the longest scenic byway

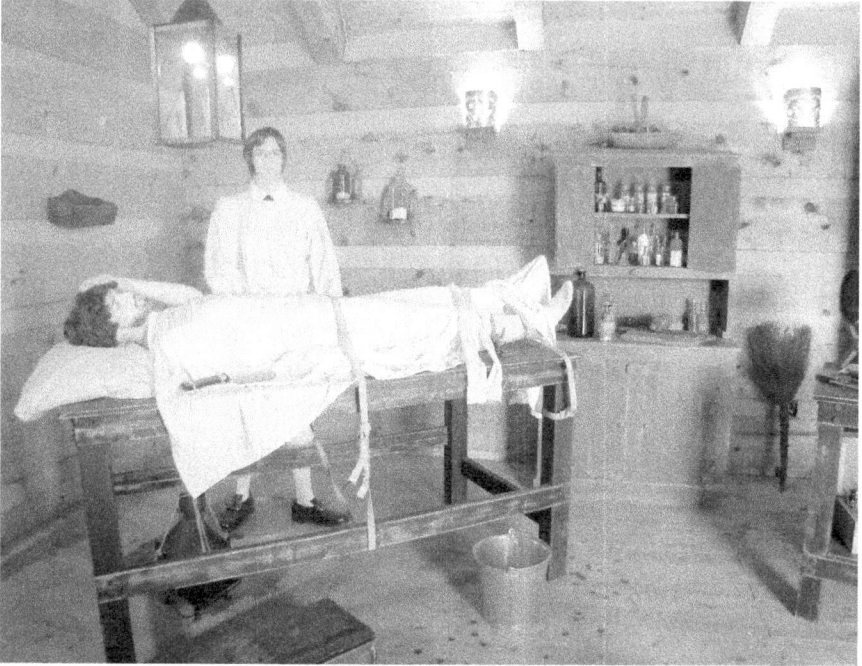

Dr. John Elliott's surgery as it might have looked at Fort Steuben's hospital. The hospital is not shown in the January 1787 sketch but may have been added later.

in the United States), making the project eligible for federal moneys. The facility would be known as the "Eastern Gateway Visitor's Center."

On July 24, 2002, ground was broken for the new park and the five-thousand-square-foot visitors' center. After a year of construction and landscaping, the grand opening was held June 1, 2003, and a dedication ceremony on June 14. Ribbons were cut, balloons were released and the twenty-foot-high fountain was turned on. "This is the gem of downtown Steubenville," Elizabeth King told the well-wishers who attended the celebration. "The entire town has been extremely supportive."

That September marked yet another bicentennial: the 200th anniversary of Meriwether Lewis's arrival in Steubenville as part of the Lewis and Clark "Voyage of Discovery." His keelboats reached Steubenville on September 6, 1803, and so the crew retracing the expedition visited Fort Steuben September 6 and 7, 2003, bringing their keelboat replicas with them on the Ohio. Lewis had not intended to stay in Steubenville, but they stuck on a sandbar (or "riffle," as Lewis called it) and had to find a farmer with a strong ox to pull it free. This is how the Lewis and Clark journal recorded the event:

Rebuilding Fort Steuben

Struck on a riffle about two miles below the town hoisted our mainsail to assist in driving us over the riffle the wind blew so heard as to break the spreat of it, and now having no assistance but by manual exertion and my men woarn down by perpetual lifting I was obliged again to have recourse to my usual resort and sent out in serch of horses or oxen—Stewbenville a small town situated on the Ohio in the state of Ohio about six miles above Charlestown in Virginia and 24 above Wheeling—is small well built thriving place has several respectable families residing in it, five years since it was a wilderness—the oxen arrived got off with difficulty the oxen drew badly however with their assistance we got over two other riffles which lyed just below; we preceeded about a mile and a half further and encamped on the west bank—having made ten miles *this day.*

The Corps of Discovery and the Army Corps of Engineers used the opportunity to place a GPS beacon at Fort Steuben bearing the insignia of Lewis and Clark's Corps of Discovery—crossed peace pipes and a friendly hand shake—reproducing the engraving on the medals given as peace offerings to the Indians encountered on the voyage.

With the Eastern Gateway Visitor's Center making the park a year-round commitment, the Old Fort Steuben Project recognized the need for a full-time director of the fort. In March 2004, Judy Bratten became executive director of Fort Steuben and began scheduling year-round activities related to history—not just local history, and not just fort-era history, but anything

GPS marker for Fort Steuben, engraved with the Lewis and Clark Voyage of Discovery emblem.

educational that sent the message that Fort Steuben would be a center of the pursuit of history. The following year, construction began on the Louis and Sandra Berkman Amphitheater, a three-hundred-seat outdoor concert venue behind the visitors' center. Since its opening, the amphitheater has been the home of a free concert series supported by grants and corporate and private donations. The free concerts are a way for Fort Steuben to give something back to the town that supported its reconstruction from the start.

In August 2009, the Fort Steuben Eastern Gateway Visitor's Center received national recognition at the National Scenic Byways Conference in Denver, Colorado. Sponsored by America's Byways Resource Center, the Federal Highway Administration and the American Association of State Highway and Transportation Officials (AASHTO), the conference gave Fort Steuben's center one of eight awards nationally, honoring it for its excellence in four criteria: community involvement and outreach; partnerships; advancing the goals of the byway's Corridor Management Plan; and innovation. "This award," wrote Judy Bratten, "is a fitting acknowledgement of the outstanding work that was accomplished by the original Fort Steuben Project Committee, especially Elizabeth King and her late husband, Richard, and the continued efforts of our Board and volunteers to make Historic Fort Steuben an outstanding landmark and educational center for the community and the surrounding area."

In November 2009, construction began on the last remaining structure of the Fort Steuben reconstruction: the guard tower and sally port. The gate facing the river had been built in the 1990s without incorporating the guardhouse, simply because there were not sufficient funds to build it. In a decade of weathering, many of the pickets needed replacing, so it was a perfect time to build the additional structure, which the 1787 sketch shows was part of the original fort.

The Eastern Gateway Visitor's Center, including Fort Steuben (left) and the red-roofed Berkman Amphitheater (far right).

Rebuilding Fort Steuben

And so, after a little more than twenty years of construction, Fort Steuben—the second incarnation of Fort Steuben—was finally complete. The fortunate fluke of obtaining the very site of its original construction and turning it into a beautiful park in the center of downtown Steubenville was matched by another fluke: winding up adjacent to the other most famous artifact of the area's earliest history, the first federal land office.

While Fort Steuben is a meticulously accurate reconstruction, based on original sketches, the land office is in fact the original building, constructed in 1801 and used to record land deeds for the first federal land sales district until 1840. The story of how it ended up in its present location next to Fort Steuben (or vice versa, since the land office was there first) is an odd one.

On May 12, 1800, President John Adams appointed David Hoge of Philadelphia the first registrar of the Federal Land Office, the government body designated to record land deeds for the western expansion of the United States. Since the land sales had begun in the Seven Ranges measured by the surveyors protected by Fort Steuben, Adams decided that the "Steubenville District" should be the starting point of land sales in the nineteenth century. In 1801, Hoge built a one-room log cabin to serve as both his home and recording office. He built it on Third Street, lot 104, about where the Steubenville Post Office is now. In 1809, Hoge moved the land office to lot 113, still on Third Street but now north of Washington, where it remained for twelve years. The cabin was small enough that Hoge probably found it easier simply to dismantle and reassemble the timbers rather than rebuild. In 1821, the building was moved to the northeast corner of Market and Alley A (now Court Street). In 1828, Hoge dismantled it again and moved it to South Third Street between Market and Adams. This was its final move for more than a century, since the little timber structure was bricked up and covered with a larger brick building. Not until the outer building was torn down in 1941 did people discover that the original beams of the 1801 house were preserved inside the brick walls of the building now scheduled for demolition.

A few civic-minded people, realizing what they had discovered, tried to save the building. Eventually, they found space for it outside of town, in what is now Steubenville's "West End," near what would today be the campus of Eastern Gateway Community College. There it was used as a plane-spotting station during World War II. It remained a tourist attraction until 1963, when the cabin had to be moved again to accommodate the widening of Route 22. This time the history-minded leaders of Steubenville wanted to bring this piece of its past closer to its original home. The nearest strip of land vacant and controlled by the city was right on Route 7 near the

The first federal land office, built in 1801, was the nation's first registry of land sold outside of the original thirteen states. *Courtesy First Federal Land Office.*

Fort Steuben Bridge. Then, in 1976, it was Route 7's turn to be widened, displacing the little cabin again. It moved farther south, still on Route 7, until *that* space was needed for the University Boulevard interchange for the new Veteran's Memorial Bridge in 1983. Finally, Ohio Power found a home for it in the corner of its lot, exactly as it would do a few years later for Fort Steuben. Since 1989, the fort and the land office have been neighbors.

Bill Croskey, the curator of the land office, likes to tell the story of Bazaleel Wells, the surveyor of Steubenville, buying the first lots that would become Steubenville from Hoge. "He gave those first five acres to the city that he founded, and they put the courthouse on it and that is where it stands today," Croskey told the *Herald Star* in a 1997 interview for the city's bicentennial. His reason for emphasizing the courthouse was that the current courthouse originally had a distinctive bell tower, which was damaged in a snowstorm in the 1950s and had to be removed. The 5,700-pound bell was no longer safe on the roof, so it got shuffled around (how many places can accommodate a two-and-a-half-ton bell?) until it finally found a home in front of the land office. It is still there and is occasionally rung, to the delight of the school groups that visit the land office.

A TOUR OF HISTORIC FORT STEUBEN

THE BLOCKHOUSES

The reconstructed Fort Steuben as it stands today is scrupulously modeled on the detailed 1787 sketch saved from Major Beatty's papers, in regard to dimension and layout. It does not, however, slavishly follow eighteenth-century standards in terms of comfort. The struggle to balance both in a facility designed for twenty-first-century visitors is not an easy one. Electrical outlets, light switches and baseboard heating are made as inconspicuous as possible. Even the cement-block foundation for each building is a compromise with authenticity; there would have been no such foundation on the original fort. But without it on the modern fort, the beams would rot from the ground up. Who in their right mind would insure a structure whose builders didn't even take the simplest precautions to protect it? And so a modern reconstruction must have a basement, even if the original did not. And so, invariably, visitors see the trapdoor to the basement and imagine secret passages or hidden storage for valuables. And the interpreters have to explain something that probably would not have been there in the original.

Now that you have met the people who made the original Fort Steuben—the soldiers, the squatters and the surveyors, as well as the Native Americans who came before them—and now that the reconstructed fort is complete, let's take a tour of the finished product as it looks in 2010, much like its 1787 original, but speaking to the twenty-first century. If you have not seen the fort, you can refer to that 1787 sketch made by Lieutenant Ebenezer Frothingham and orient it by the compass. The sally port and guard tower face the river; that is the eastern wall of the compound. Going clockwise,

A Fort Steuben blockhouse in winter. The water barrels were placed under the eaves, pitched to maximize runoff, conserving rainwater in case of siege.

then, on the southern wall we find the artificer's shop to the east and the quartermaster's store to the west. The western wall contains the two identical officers' quarters. The northern wall holds, to the west, the commissary, and to the east, the hospital, which is not shown in the 1787 sketch. Also not shown is a concession to modern regulations: modern restrooms, disguised (quite cleverly, we think) as a typical eighteenth-century building. Baron von Steuben's regulations for the first American army require simply the digging of "sinks," or pits into which to dump all of a fort's wastes. For some reason, the various government agencies that gave grants to build the visitors' center at Fort Steuben discouraged such a solution for the reconstructed fort. And so the Old Fort Steuben Project built what its late leader Dick King used to call "the most expensive bathroom in Jefferson County."

The four blockhouses are a convenient starting point for our tour, since they were the starting point of construction both in 1786 and in 1989. The blockhouses were designed as both the living quarters of the majority of the soldiers (the enlisted men) and the first line of defense in case of attack. One blockhouse occupies each of the four corners of the stockade, but at a forty-five-degree angle to it. The blockhouses were literally blocks: exactly twenty-five feet square on the inside of the bottom portion and twenty-eight feet square on the outside—making the walls eighteen inches thick. The upper story, however, makes a larger square, so there is an overhang, and on top of that a steeply pitched roof. The roof in the upper story begins only four feet from the floor, but the pitch of the roof is so steep that a fully grown soldier can stand comfortably within a foot or so of the outer wall. And since the only business he had at the outer wall was to point a musket out the gun ports, and that from a kneeling position, the design was functional.

Every aspect of this design is functional, and just as a surveyor's mind thinks in terms of geometry, so too does the eighteenth-century soldier's. No wonder the two groups got on so well together. The forty-five-degree angle of the blockhouses meant that a direct line of fire from one blockhouse would be ninety degrees from that from the adjacent blockhouse. This is the optimum crossfire, meaning that even firing randomly, the musketeers would have the highest mathematical probability of hitting any enemy advancing in the space between the blockhouses, 150 feet apart. Even that distance was designed to maximize the effectiveness of the army flintlocks, which had an effective range of just that distance. The firelocks were not rifles: the bore was smooth, reducing the accuracy of the shot. That does not mean that the frontier marksman could not achieve a remarkable degree of accuracy with the weapon; they could and did. But the strategy of firing by volley in which American troops were trained, thanks to Baron von Steuben, was again geometric: covering the field with a grid of flying lead to maximize the damage to the enemy.

That sort of battle, however, firing from the gun ports of the second story, did not happen in the seven months of Fort Steuben's active life. If the soldier was in the blockhouse at all, he was on the first floor and probably in bed. The barracks would have been relatively crowded. Hamtramck's description in his December 15, 1786 letter to Harmar describes the blockhouses as partitioned down the middle, with a central double-chimney and a hearth facing the center of either partition, with fourteen men on either side. Fourteen men in a space a little more than twenty-five by twelve and a half feet. Their meager rations (when Daniel Britt would send them, or if Andrew van Swearingen had a good day hunting) could be cooked over the central fireplace.

Whisky was allotted to the men, as we have already seen, though strictly rationed. Exceptions to that rationing included the prize for the completion of the blockhouses, mentioned above, and perhaps holidays. Christmas

Close-up of the fireplace in one of the blockhouses.

and New Year's are the ones that first come to mind, but in nearby Fort McIntosh, Major William Denny in his diary described whisky as a major element of a holiday that fell on March 17, 1786:

> *A majority of the men in garrison are Irish. The soldiers requested to have the privilege of celebrating this day, as was customary. Accordingly the bung was opened and every man had permission to purchase and drink what quantity of liquor he pleased; and a pretty good portion did some of them take, for toward the evening we had not six men in the garrison fit for duty, not even the guard excepted.*

The entry for the next day was instructive and, if you'll excuse the phrase, sobering: "G. Palfrey died from the effects of too much liquor—and was buried the next day."

Payday was also an occasion to allow extra rum, but the soldier had to pay for it. This is Denny's description of the aftermath of payday, March 3–5, 1786:

> *After they had laid out the greatest part of their settlements for dry goods, reserving only a small share for liquor, they got permission to purchase the same, and toleration to get drunk, so that it would not interfere with their duty; but this charge had no effect; for three days there was scarcely one sober man in the garrison, and God knows how long they would have continued so, if the issues had not been stopped. So between the wet and dry affairs, Captain O'Hara will take nearly the same sum of money back that he brought, except what the officers received.*

While this was the scene at McIntosh, only fifteen miles away, and in the same western army, Fort Steuben was likely to be similar. Though perhaps not. Captain Hamtramck had a reputation for running a tight ship. In complaining about the shoddy accounting he found in most companies on

Soldiers were responsible for upkeep and replacement of equipment issued to them, such as this haversack and canteen. Powder horns were less common, since soldiers pre-made cartridges.

the frontier, Denny singled out Hamtramck as an exception. "Receiving and digesting the monthly returns of the troops at all these different posts, was a business of some trouble," Denny wrote in February 1787. "Those from the post commanded by Hamtramck less difficulty with. Colonel Harmar thinks him one of his best captains."

The soldiers' pay was meager in 1787 and had not been increased as inflation of the American dollar soared due to the war debt. Privates and corporals were paid four dollars a month; fifers and drummers got five and sergeants six. Furthermore, they had to replace out of their pay any supplies issued to them that were lost or prematurely worn—hence the big set-to over the woolen britches. Baron von Steuben's manual of arms lists the following "stoppages"—that is, money taken out of their pay—assessed to soldiers for their armaments:

Firelock $16.00
Bayonet $2.00
Ramrod $1.00
Cartridge Box $4.00
Bayonet Belt $1.00
Scabbard $2/3
Cartridge $1/6
Flint $1/20
Gun-worm $¼
Screwdriver $1/12

Because Captain Hamtramck dealt directly with his officers and not with non-coms (the familiar abbreviation for "noncommissioned officer" was current in Hamtramck's day and appears in his writing), we know the names of all 12 officers of Fort Steuben but virtually none of the 12 sergeants, 11 corporals or 135 privates. Only one name appears for an enlisted man, Sergeant Easton, and he is mentioned only because he carried messages for his commander. We know nothing more about him, not even his first name. And isn't that always the way? The enlisted men are the anonymous ones in military history.

THE OFFICERS' QUARTERS

The visitors to Fort Steuben who are the most impressed by the officers' quarters are usually the ones who have seen the enlisted men's barracks—

the blockhouses—first. As Spartan as the accommodations for captains and lieutenants seem by modern standards, the dormitories of Fort Steuben's officers seem positively luxurious and spacious when compared to where the privates lived. The table of organization for a company called for only three officers: a captain in command, one lieutenant and one ensign. That makes only nine officers for two buildings. But other functions at the fort required officers: the commissary, the quartermaster and the company surgeon (which was a rank in itself, at a pay grade equal to a major). That makes an even dozen, and that's exactly what we find reflected in Hamtramck's letters: four captains (Hamtramck himself, McCurdy, Mercer and the commissary, Miller), four lieutenants (Bissell, Frothingham, Kersey and the quartermaster, Peters), three ensigns (Armstrong, Luse and Seydam) and one surgeon (Dr. Elliott). So there were probably only six officers in each of the buildings.

The front door of the officers' barracks opens into a parlor where guests were entertained (which, even on the frontier, was not as rare as we might think; the officers kept contact with the farmers and local officials on the Virginia side). The table would sit six comfortably and would have been set more elegantly than we might imagine. Each officer was assigned a packhorse in addition to his mount, and whatever the horse could carry came with him. China and silver were probably not out of the question. The right rear corner of the parlor opened into a kitchen where an enlisted man cooked for the officers.

To the left were the officers' dorms, just enough space for a few beds. The commander, of course, had a private room; Hamtramck most likely had the only private room in the fort. The bed in the reconstruction is canopied, which was a likely precaution, not so much for privacy as for warmth. Hamtramck would have had a desk for the constant paperwork that has always been the bane of army life (though, as historians, we are grateful for that paperwork; it allows us to reconstruct the soldier's daily life). His campaign chest, or military footlocker, would have become another piece of furniture when he was not on the march. To the great fortune of Fort Steuben, Hamtramck's actual military chest survives in the West Point Museum at Olmsted Hall in the U.S. Military Academy. The museum graciously shared dimensions and photos of the box with Andy Celestin, Fort Steuben's own woodcraft artisan, and Andy reproduced it with aged, weathered barn wood.

The officers, of course, also fared better than the "regulars" on payday. An ensign collected twenty dollars a month, a lieutenant twenty-six and a captain thirty-five. Dr. Elliott's pay as surgeon was forty-five dollars, equal to a major's. But captains had to make up any shortages in their company, which is why a good officer kept a good inventory.

Captain Hamtramck's military chest—an exact replica of the original in the West Point Museum, U.S. Military Academy.

THE QUARTERMASTER'S STORE

The noun "store" has shifted meaning slightly since the Fort Steuben days. Today, we think of a "store" as a place to buy things, but of course it attained that meaning from its original sense (a place to keep things) by a very natural process: if you want to buy something, you go to where it is kept. In 1787, the word was already shifting to its modern sense, and when the quartermaster's store was reconstructed at the modern Fort Steuben in 1996, Steubenville *Herald Star* reporter Mark Law had fun on the dual sense of the word in his October 5 headline: "New Store Coming to Steubenville."

The quartermaster was responsible for keeping all non-food items not in actual use. His accounts had to balance, so he would always insist on a receipt for any item deposited or withdrawn. The tally was a constant concern at Fort Steuben because of the failures of the contractor, or "provisioner," Daniel Britt, to fill his orders. Captain Hamtramck would often have to procure items from stores at other posts, and the quartermasters there were not always as scrupulous with their receipts as Hamtramck demanded his own quartermaster to be. His August 16, 1786 report to Colonel Harmar complained of just such an exchange with Captain William Ferguson, quartermaster at Fort McIntosh:

> *I also in Consequence of your Orders of the 19th of July send a Monthly Return of the troops, and one of Military Store to Major Doughty. The later one may with probability Not agree with the last Inspection Return, for the troops have been made Compleat to 29 Cartriges for Each Man and the remaining ammunition has ben sent to McIntosh. We have sent all our Cloathing to Fort all Intact but Capt Furgeson Refused to Give a Receipt.*

Individual soldier's equipment on hand in the quartermaster's store at Fort Steuben include bayonet bolts, bayonet scabbards, gun slings, gun worms (an implement for drawing unfired cartridges or wadding from a gun barrel), swords, haversacks, knapsacks, canteens and camp kettles. Clothing items included (when in supply) hats, coats, vests, britches, shirts, gloves, stockings,

The quartermaster's store contained all non-food items belonging to the regiment but not yet in use.

shoes, shoe buckles, blankets, linen overalls and woolen overalls. For camp equipage, there were three kinds of tents, axes, axe slings, watches, steel mallets, spades, shovels and pickaxes. Under the category "Arms, Accessories, and Ammunition" was listed officer's fusees (a signal flare, though the word was also an archaic term for a flintlock), muskets, scabbards, fifes, drums, flints and cartridges.

There is no indication of what carpenter's tools were on hand, possibly because they followed whatever company or detachment was building the next fort. But at least at the time Fort Steuben was built, the quartermaster's store must have had something like this list credited to a detachment under Captain Heart in a return dated April 24, 1787: one eight-ounce barrel of twine, one whipsaw, one crosscut saw, one handsaw, two broad axes, twenty falling axes, ten fascine hatchets, fifteen spades, two adzes, five shovels, ten picks, nine iron squares, one pair of compasses, two crowbars, two draw knives, one pair of iron wedges, one jack plain wedge, one long plain wedge, three augurs, two hammers, two spike gimlets, six gimlets, two chisels, one pair of tongs, one grindstone, two fascine hooks and two stone hammers.

One non-food supply that was in constant demand at the quartermaster's store—because many of them were expended every night—was candles. Hamtramck's long-undelivered contractor's shipment of August 1786 included three ninety-nine-pound boxes of candles. A look at any of the rooms in any of the buildings at Fort Steuben will show us why. In addition to the large chandelier (which we now think of as an electric source of illumination, but the word comes from "candle") in the officers' quarters, virtually every wall of every room has at least one candleholder, and there are candles on Hamtramck's desk for his endless paperwork.

The quartermaster at Fort Steuben was Lieutenant William Peters, like most of the officers at Fort Steuben a veteran of the Revolution. Peters had served in the Second New York Continental Infantry, and his commission in the federal period was dated June 27, 1786, which means that Fort Steuben was his very first military assignment in the federal army. Until October 1786, Peters served on the range lines with everybody else, since there was no permanent quartermaster's store in the wilderness. Once the store was in place, however, it was virtually Peters's home from December 1786, to May 1787.

At times, especially just after payday, the kind of store where you keep things became the kind of store where you buy things. When the contractor came through, he would sometimes become almost a frontier peddler, "spreading his blanket," as the traders say, in the quartermaster's store. For this reason, the quartermaster's store at the reconstructed Fort Steuben shows examples of the most common trade good on the Ohio in 1787: furs. Major Denny describes one of the "sale days" of Fort McIntosh contractor Captain James O'Hara (who six years later would go as high in the quartermaster world as a man could go by becoming quartermaster general of the United States in 1792). O'Hara was engaged at the time in supplying trade goods to the Ohio nations to build goodwill during the surveying. "Major Finney," Denny reported in his journal, "commenced the payment, and Captain O'Hara opened a cheap assortment of goods, which he disposed of to the soldiers as quick as they received their money."

The quartermaster's duties went beyond keeping items, however. In a real sense, he performed the function of a medieval steward who saw to the day-to-day logistics of a nobleman's estate. Lieutenant Peters did that for Fort Steuben. Baron von Steuben's description of the quartermaster's responsibilities might stagger a mere mortal:

> *The quarter-master, being charged with encamping and quartering the regiment, should be at all times acquainted with its strength, that he may require no more ground than is necessary, nor have more tents pitched than the number prescribed; for both [of] which he is responsible.*

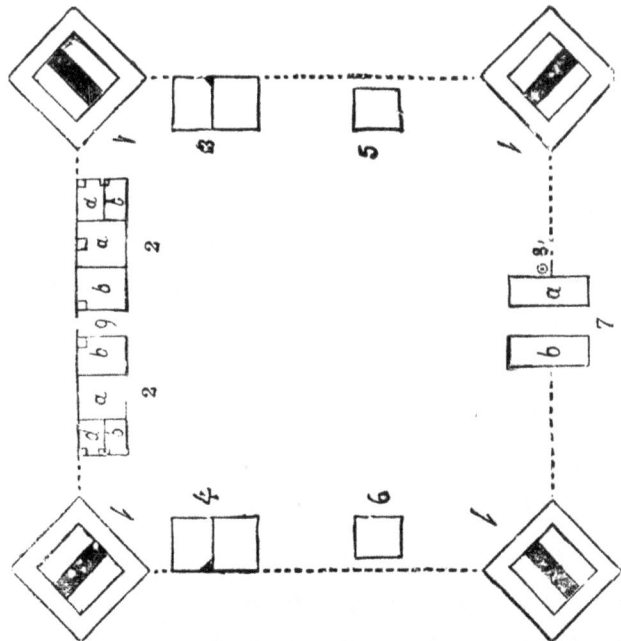

This sketch of Fort Steuben was made by Lieutenant Ebenezer Frothingham shortly after the fort was completed on January 8, 1787.

He must inform the regiment where to fetch their wood, water and other necessaries, and where to pasture the horses.

He must instruct the quarter-master serjeant and pioneers in the manner of laying out the camp, agreeable to the order prescribed in the regulations.

He is answerable to the cleanliness of the camp, and that the soldiers make no fire any where but in the kitchens.

When the army marches, he must conduct the pioneers to the place appointed, and order the quarter-master serjeant to take charge of the baggage.

He is to make out all returns for camp equipage, arms, accoutrements, ammunition, provisions, and forage, and receive and distribute them to the regiment, taking the necessary vouchers for the delivery, and entering all receipts and deliveries in a book kept by him for that purpose.

He must pay particular attention to the preservation of camp equipage, cause the necessary repairs to be done when wanting, and return every thing unfit for use to the stores from which he drew them.

The preservation of arms, accoutrements and ammunition is of such essential importance, that he must be strictly attentive to have those of the sick, of the men on furlough, discharged, or detached on command without arms, taken care of and deposited with the brigade conductor, as directed in the regulations.

One cannot help but wonder if Lieutenant Peters ever slept.

THE COMMISSARY'S STORE

Whether or not it was because of the uncertainty of the supplies from contractor Daniel Britt of Turnbull & Marmie's Pittsburgh office, Fort Steuben had three different commissaries in its brief life (the officer, that is, not the building; there was only one of those). Captain John Mills was the commissary when the companies first arrived at the surveyors' camp in September 1786. Virtually as soon as he had a building, however, the first of the year 1787, Mills transferred to an artillery unit, and Fort Steuben needed a new commissary officer.

Lieutenant William Peters was Fort Steuben's commissary for only about a month, early January to February 8, 1787. On that day, a civilian, John Matthews, took over the job. The commissary was another store, this one exclusively for food items. Hamtramck's Fort Steuben papers do not include commissary returns—not surprising, considering Britt's bad track record with Fort Steuben. But returns from Forts Harmar and Finney from the same period show the kinds of supplies commissaries would have on hand.

Meat, of course, was a big part of the soldier's diet, but hard to keep fresh a century and a half before artificial refrigeration. One method of ensuring fresh meat was the way that Hamtramck brought beef to the site of Fort Steuben: on the hoof. The commissary was responsible for the camp's abattoir, or slaughtering place, as Baron von Steuben noted in his military manual: "The place where the cattle are killed must be at least fifty paces in the rear of the wagons; and the entrails and other filth immediately buried; for which the commissaries are answerable."

But another common way of preserving meat on the Ohio frontier was setting up a smoker. Captain Walter Finney's return for August 26, 1786, from the fort that bears his name reports twenty-nine pounds of beef "on the scaffold smoking" and another fifteen pounds already smoked. "The beef was spoiling very fast," Finney noted, "and I have put the whole to smoke in order to preserve it." A third method of preservation was in brine, like corned beef. Another return from Fort Finney for the same day lists ten bushels of salt. The phantom shipment from contractor Daniel Britt that was delayed almost a month, bringing many soldiers on the line close to starving, contained, in addition to the twenty head of cattle, twenty-eight tunnes of salt beef. A tunne was a large cask equal to 252 gallons liquid measure. If these quantities seem large, remember that they were feeding over 150 men doing hard work. The rule of thumb for the army, according to estimates Captain Hutchins made during the French and Indian War, was a pound and a half per man per day.

None of the soldiers at Fort Steuben found themselves relishing the prospect of eating panther, as Winthrop Sargent found himself doing on the trail, but often there, as on the ranges, they were obliged to eat what the hunters could supply. Usually, of course, this was venison, because anything smaller would not feed that many men. But wild turkey was also common and relatively easy to hunt. Major Denny describes hunting turkey Shawnee style on New Year's Eve 1785:

> I set out in company with two Shawanees to provide a few turkeys for the first of the year, and at the request of General Parsons, agreed to meet him, General Butler and Major Finney, at a large pond about six miles up the river; they to go in a boat. After we had rode the distance of four or five miles (for our party was all on horse-back; I was mounted on one of the

The officers' mess in the parlor of the officers' quarters was more pleasantly presented than the open-fire cooking in the blockhouses.

Indians' wife's horse and saddle), we got amongst the turkeys; and the first thing done was to charge *upon them, so as to cause them to fly up on the trees, and all the howlings and frightful screeches I ever heard, were given to effect this purpose. As soon as the turkeys rose we alighted and commenced firing. In this manner we sported with two flocks, until we had as many as we could conveniently carry home.*

The kinds of storable dried foods we expect to find in a fort—beans and peas, for example—are not mentioned. But there was almost always flour, in large quantities, converted regularly into biscuits for the troops. Captain Walter Finney's receipt to Captain Hamtramck for supplies transferred from Fort Finney in August 1786 itemizes forty barrels and thirty-six kegs of flour, totaling 11,860 pounds.

The Artificer's Shop

Every town in the eighteenth century had at least one blacksmith's shop. But the western army had to carry its own with it, since a broken ramrod, horseshoe or any metal implement had to be replaced quickly with an army on the move. As soon as Hamtramck's three companies had a permanent home, the soldiers built a shop for Fort Steuben's blacksmith—"artificer" was the military term, since his job was to make things—and also, because he may not always work in iron, the "black" metal (so called because of the black fire scale that builds up on wrought iron when heated).

The artificer was usually an enlisted man, one of the 135 anonymous men of Fort Steuben, so we don't know his name—in fact, there could have been more than one artificer. The shop was pretty spare, even by the standards of 1787. We don't have a list of the Fort Steuben artificer's equipment, but as with so many other aspects of Fort Steuben, we can reconstruct from the equipment of similar forts at the same time. Captain Jonathan Heart's company artificer claimed the following items on April 24, 1787:

1 Pair Bellows
1 Anvil
1 Sledge
1 pair tongs
1 hammer
1 Vice
10 pounds of steel
100 pounds of iron in store

The portability of this equipment was crucial on the frontier, and particularly on this mission, because at the beginning of the surveying in the summer of 1786, most of the three companies were on the ranges, and a smithying need was more likely to arise in the woods—where iron wedges and "falling axes" were testing their temper against trees—than in the geographer's camp, where life was more sedentary. The importance of the artificer can be gauged by the fact that he was the subject of conflicting demands by the troops on the Ohio. On July 19, Colonel Harmar ordered Hamtramck to send the artificer to Fort Harmar. Nearly a month later, on August 16, Hamtramck was constrained to explain his noncompliance: "The artificer is out on Command, which is the Reason why I have not sent him agreeable to your order."

Fort Steuben's artificer's shop had a portable forge and anvil, as pictured here, and could repair or fabricate most metal implements needed by the army.

Even though Hamtramck built Fort Steuben as if it were to be a permanent post, he was fortunate even to have an artificer's shop. Captain Walter Finney wrote his August 26, 1786 letter to Colonel Harmer with this postscript: "Note—a Traveling Forge would be of Infinite advantage at this Post." No doubt Captain Hamtramck found it so at Fort Steuben.

THE HOSPITAL

"There is nothing which gains an officer the love of his soldiers more," wrote Baron von Steuben in the first *American Manual of Arms*, "than his care of them under the distress of sickness; it is then he has the power of exerting his humanity in providing them everything necessary, and making their situation as agreeable as possible." The baron's description of the layout of a military camp emphasizes the importance of care for the sick but also raises a question for the reconstruction of Fort Steuben. "Two or three tents," he wrote, "should be set apart in every regiment for the reception of such sick as cannot be sent to the general hospital, or whose cases may not require it."

Clearly, there should be a "general hospital," even where there are sick tents. Why, then, is there no hospital shown on the 1787 sketch of the fort? It may simply be that the sketch was made before the hospital was built. It was Paymaster Beatty's February 6, 1787 visit to Fort Steuben that occasioned his taking possession of the sketch, which may have been made earlier—though not more than a month earlier, since Hamtramck reports the fort finished on January 8. It is, of course, possible that the hospital was never built. The baron's regulations make it clear that a regiment should have a hospital, but Fort Steuben's three companies were not a complete regiment—the infantry regiment was scattered along the Ohio, and its headquarters, Fort Harmar, had its own hospital. Fort Steuben did have its own surgeon, however, and it would be surprising if it did not have at least a small infirmary.

It may even be argued that Dr. John Elliott was the first medical man in Ohio. Born in New York, where he received his medical training at King's College (later Columbia), he volunteered as a surgeon's mate to a New York regiment as soon as the Revolution began. He retained that rank when the new federal army was established in 1785 but was promoted to the surgeoncy the following year—and his first assignment as full surgeon was to Captain Hamtramck's unit. Hamtramck's detachment orders for the first groups going into the woods required Dr. Elliott's oversight. Item twelve of his September 1, 1786 orders told each commander of a detachment: "You will call on Doctor Elliot who will give you medicines for the use of your men and Direction how to take them."

Thanks to the army's mandate for monthly inspections (and Hamtramck's excellent record keeping), we know precisely what kind of equipment and pharmaceuticals Dr. Elliott carried into the Ohio frontier. Surgical instruments were not listed, but since dental instruments were ("1 sett tooth instruments"), it is more likely that Elliott brought his own than that he cared for 150 men without them. Of the forty-one medications listed, many might today be considered herbal remedies, but many are medications we still use. Military reenactors who have visited the reconstructed Fort Steuben often assume that anesthesia on the frontier was limited to a shot of whiskey and a bullet to bite on. But, in fact, Dr. Elliott carried two powerful opiates: *tintura thebaica*, a form of laudanum, or opium dissolved in alcohol, and *gummi opii*, "opium gum," poppy resin that was almost pure opium.

Dr. Elliott, like many American physicians, was not as reluctant as might be supposed to learn remedies from Native Americans. From the Lenape,

Dr. Elliott's pharmacy contained virtually any medication needed on the frontier.

frontiersmen in western Pennsylvania had learned to crush the bark of the white poplar to make an effective cough suppressant. The scientists called it *pulvis cortex populus*, but that's just Latin for "powdered bark of poplar." From the other Indians—the ones in India—Elliott had Indian snakeroot, a powerful sedative. For fainting, Elliott used the most common European remedy, hartshorn, an aqueous ammonia solution derived, as the popular name (and its Latin scientific equivalent, *spiritus cornu cervi*) suggests, from the antlers of deer.

Other medications on hand included the following. The first name given is the standard, usually Latin, abbreviation exactly as Dr. Elliott recorded it in his return for January 27, 1787; in parentheses afterward is the expanded form of the Latin name, followed by a modern name (if there is one) and a brief explanation.

Crem: Tart *(cream of tartar, modern potassium bitartrate, a byproduct of wine fermentation used as a laxative)*

Cantharides *(the so-called "Spanish fly," made from the exoskeletons of beetles; contrary to myth, not an aphrodisiac, but an anti-irritant)*

Flor: Sulph *(flower of sulfur: fine powder produced by condensation of sulfur, used to kill internal parasites)*

Flor: Cham *(flower of chamomile: a sedative)*

Sal Epsom *(Epsom salts = magnesium sulfate, an emetic)*

Sal Martis *("green vitriol" = ferrous sulfate, used to treat iron deficient anemia)*

Sal Absinth *(sal absinthii, an impure potassium carbonate from ashes of wormwood, used as a "stomachic," or appetite inducer)*

Gum Camphor *(stimulant, expectorant, diaphoretic)*

Gum Ammon *(gum ammoniac, an expectorant)*

Gum Opii *(gummi opii = "opium gum" = resin from poppies, used as a pain reliever)*

Gum Arabic *(acacia, an emulsifier for keeping other medicines in suspension)*

Sperma Ceti *(whale oil for making ointments)*

Mer: Dulcis *(mercurius dulcis "sweet mercury" = calomel, used to treat constipation)*

Mer: precip: Rub *(mercurius precip. ruber, red oxide of mercury, used to treat eczema)*

Mer: Corros Sublim *(mercurius corrosivus = Mercuric Chloride, used for bladder problems or venereal disease)*

Vitriol Cerul *(copper sulfate, "blue vitriol," used as an emetic, to induce vomiting)*

Vitriol Alb *("white vitriol," now known as zinc sulfate, an emetic, or an astringent to shrink body tissue, useful to close wounds)*

Tart: Emet *(tartar emetic: bitartrate of potash, crystals that form in wine casks during fermentation, used as an expectorant and to treat parasitic infections)*

Rad: serpt *(radix serpentine = rauvolfia serpentinae radix = Indian snakeroot; used as sedative and as cure for bites)*

Rad: Gentian *(radix gentian = rhizome and root of gentian, used as tonic)*

Ars Alb *(arsenic alba = white arsenic = an oxide of arsenic used to treat stomach upset, sore throat)*

Ung^t Mercur: Nit *(unguentum mercurii nitrate = ointment of mercury nitrate, disinfectant for gangrenous wound)*

Emp^l Cummin *(Emplastrum cymini = cumin plaster, a stimulant plaster)*

Emp^l Mercur *(emplastrum mercurii = mercury plaster, applied to small pox or other pustules)*

Elix. Vitriol *(elixir of vitriol = aromatic sulphuric acid—diluted, used to treat diarrhea)*

Sp^t Nitri Duli *(spiritus nitri dulcis = ethyl nitrate $C_2H_5NO_2$; diaphoretic, to induce sweating; diuretic, to induce urination; antispasmodic)*

Sp^t Terrabinth *(spiritus terebinth = turpentine, used topically for wounds, or mixed with fat for a chest rub)*

Ol: Lini *(oleum lini = linseed oil, used for balms for inflamed skin)*

Sp^t cornu Cervi *(spiritus cornu cervi = "hartshorn": aqueous ammonia solution, stimulant for fainting)*

Tinct: Thebaic *(tincture thebaica—a form of laudanum, opium— for pain)*

1 Sett Tooth Instruments

1 Tourniquet

6 Bandages

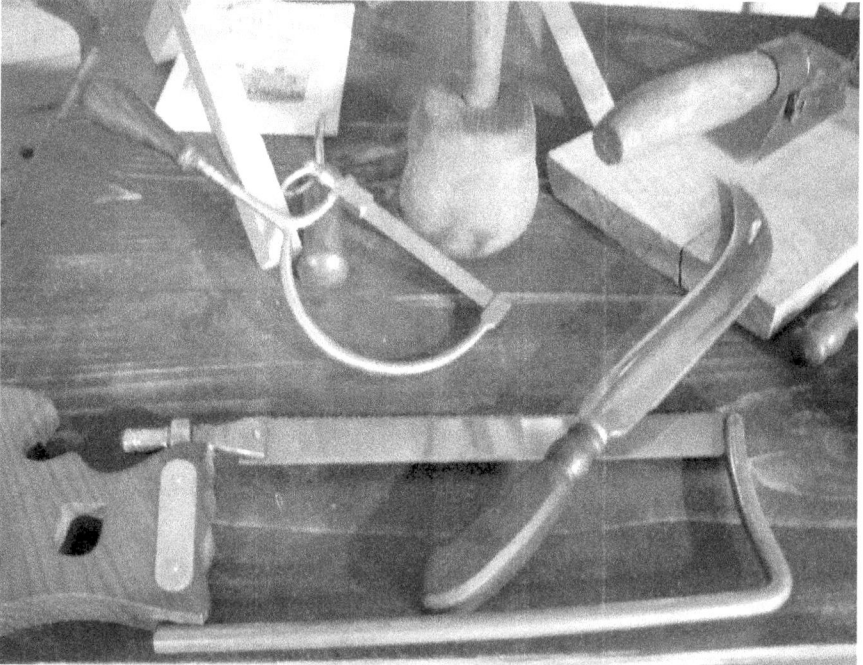

Medical instruments of the Fort Steuben era, as found in Dr. Elliott's hospital.

Dr. Elliott, a long way from New York, remained a frontier doctor the rest of his life. He followed Hamtramck's three companies down the river, but when Fort Washington was built in 1789 in what is now Cincinnati, he ran the hospital there until that fort was decommissioned in 1802. At that time he came to Dayton, where he set up a private practice until his death in 1809.

THE GUARDHOUSE

The reason Captain Hamtramck chose the second rise above the river for the site of Fort Steuben was its commanding view of the river, up and down. An elevation above that rise, then, would be even better. That is the function of the guardhouse. The structure is described thus in the "Explanation" below the 1787 sketch: "Guard House built on two Tiers, with a Piazza looking inwards, and a Sally Port between the Tiers: the Tier, a, black Hole, place of confinement...b, Common Store." The designation "Common" suggests storage not subject to the quartermaster. The "black Hole," however, was as ominous as it sounds: a stockade for prisoners, either captured enemies or the fort's own soldiers under military discipline. There is no record of any Fort Steuben soldier having been kept in the guardhouse; the only arrest recorded, that of Captain McCurdy for insubordination, sent the captain under guard to Fort McIntosh.

Not shown in the Frothingham sketch, but suggested by Hamtramck's own December 15, 1786 sketch of the fort before it was completed, is a palisade of logs running from the Sally port (the large doors through which horses may ride out) to the river. There is no indication in Hamtramck's letters that this extra defense was actually built, which is just as well for the reconstruction, since such a picket would have to go straight across Route 7, a scenario that neither the U.S. nor the Ohio Department of Transportation finds amusing.

Even without the protective walls, goods would have been fairly easily unloaded from flatboats or keelboats just 120 yards below the guardhouse and carried up to the Sally port. As Jack Boyde pointed out in his initial research for the archaeological digs, there is a discrepancy in the early accounts, some saying 60 yards and some 120. Boyde favored the 120-yard figure, which squares better with the topographical description. Since it was the soldiers and not the surveyors who built the fort, perhaps Hamtramck can be forgiven the 200 percent inaccuracy. Soldiers often gave distances in fathoms, an obsolete measure equal to two yards; Hamtramck may have

The guardhouse nearly completed, November 2009, with the Ohio River in the background.

estimated "60 fathoms" and misremembered it as sixty "yeards." If he couldn't spell "yard," we certainly can't expect him to spell "fathom."

The guardhouse was the last structure built on the reconstructed fort and, most likely, on the original fort as well. With construction now complete —after more than twenty years—where does Fort Steuben go from here? Fort Steuben's primary task is obvious: serving as a pointer to the past, as it has ever since the first blockhouse. But it is also a pointer to the future. The Eastern Gateway Visitor's Center is a frequent meeting place for entrepreneurs who would like to revitalize Steubenville's downtown. By acting as a hub for such activities, and for other civic groups, the Fort Steuben reconstruction can show Steubenville its future as well as its past. At the time of its completion with the guardhouse in 2010, the second Fort Steuben had already had a useful life thirty-five times longer than that of the original Fort Steuben. The first fort may have ended up being a temporary stop on the way to measuring America. But the second one is working on its third decade. I think it's here to stay.

A FORT STEUBEN WHO'S WHO, 1786-1787

B ecause so many of the people connected with the original Fort Steuben continued to be the movers and shakers of Ohio (and elsewhere), a great deal has been recorded about them. I have tried to include a sense of who these people were in the text, but to make sure no one gets left out, here is an alphabetical list.

Ensign John Armstrong (April 20, 1755–February 4, 1816)—born in New Jersey; enlisted with the Twenth Pennsylvania in the Revolution and later the Third Pennsylvania. In 1790, he led an attack on an Indian village on the Eel River and barely escaped with his life. Treasurer of Northwest Territory; judge in Hamilton County. Married Tabatha Goforth January 27, 1793, Hamilton, Ohio, with whom he had ten children (five boys, five girls).

Major Ekuries Beatty (October 9, 1759–February 3, 1823)—paymaster of the western army from 1786 to 1788; born in Pennsylvania, where he received his commission. He had served in the Third Pennsylvania Regiment of the Continental Infantry, commissioned lieutenant June 2, 1778; promoted brevet captain September 30, 1783. After the evacuation of Fort Steuben, Beatty was reassigned, with Captain Heart, to Arthur St. Clair's unit, but he escaped Heart's fate by a last-moment reassignment to Fort Jefferson before St. Clair's defeat at Fort Recovery, November 4, 1791. His son Charles moved to Steubenville in 1825, bringing his father's Fort Steuben papers with him.

Lieutenant Russell Bissell (January 8, 1756–September 18, 1807)—born in Bolton, Connecticut; married Eunice Rockwell in Hartford, 1783, and then settled in Manchester, Connecticut; they had four children: George

One of two identical officers' barracks at Fort Steuben, housing six officers each.

(December 26, 1784–December 23, 1829); Eunice (July 8, 1787–1860); Lewis [later major] (October 12, 1789–November 26, 1868); and Nancy (July 1795–1870). Russell Bissell died in St. Louis, Missouri.

LIEUTENANT JAMES BRADFORD (January 1, 1754–November 4, 1791)—born in Pennsylvania, commanded the New York Provincial Artillery Company from January 1776 until he was captured by the British at King's Ferry, 1779. After the war, he was attached to Harmar's artillery regiment but transferred to infantry in order to take over Mercer's company at Fort Steuben sometime in December 1786. The date of Bradford's promotion to captain is recorded as August 7, 1786, but it seems likely that he was moved up at Fort Steuben in December. He was killed by the Shawnee under Little Turtle in "St. Clair's Defeat" at Fort Recovery, November 4, 1791.

DANIEL BRITT (August 14, 1760–October 23, 1799)—born Goochland County, Virginia, moved to Pittsburgh; contractor (civilian) with Turnbull & Marmie of Philadelphia who promised but failed to supply sufficient food for the soldiers at Fort Steuben; see Hamtramck's September 3, 1786 letter to Harmar. Later served under Hamtramck (1797).

Ebenezer Buckingham—listed by Heald, *Founding of Steubenville* 1948, page 41 as one of the geographers of the Seven Ranges but not mentioned in any of the Fort Steuben documents.

Emanuel Carpenter—listed by Heald, *Founding of Steubenville* 1948, page 41 as one of the geographers of the Seven Ranges but not mentioned in any of the Fort Steuben documents.

Cox brothers (Jonathan, Friend and Israel)—came to the Ohio Valley from Brownsville, Pennsylvania, in September 1772, staking a claim in and around what is now Wellsburg by "tomahawk right," each claiming four hundred acres. Friend's portion went to his son John and William McMahon (see entry), who sold it to Charles Prather March 6, 1788, to form Charlestown (later Wellsburg). When Indian violence was threatened in 1786, van Swearingen (see entry) built "Cox's Fort," a blockhouse that apparently became a source of hospitality to the soldiers and surveyors of Fort Steuben.

Michael Duffy—one of the deputy geographers assigned to the Seven Ranges of the Northwest Ordinance; signed Hutchins's petition, October 5, 1786.

Sergeant Easton—delivered letter September 1, 1786; otherwise unknown.

Dr. John Elliott (d. 1809)—born in New York, served as surgeon's mate to the First New York Continental Infantry Regiment in the Revolution. Served as surgeon to Fort Steuben; Hamtramck's September 1, 1786 order of march directs soldiers on detachments on ranges to consult "Dr. Elliott" first. The January 27, 1787 inspection return for Fort Steuben includes Dr. Elliott's inventory of medical supplies at the fort.

Captain William Ferguson (d. 4 November 1791)—quartermaster of Fort McIntosh, summer 1786.

Lieutenant Mahlon Ford (July 26, 1756–June 12, 1820)—born in Morristown, New Jersey, served in the Second Artillery Company of the Third New Jersey Continental Infantry during the Revolution. After service in the Indian wars, Ford served at West Point, where he retired June 1, 1802.

Lieutenant Ebenezer Frothingham (January 14, 1758–October 22, 1790)—Connecticut-born officer of the First American Regiment whose drafting skills aided the surveyors in drawing the "plats," or maps of the surveyed territory. Dr. C.C. Beatty, son of Major Ekuries Beatty (see entry), asserted in 1881 that the map of Fort Steuben given him by his father was drawn by Frothingham. In the Revolution, Frothingham served in the Third Connecticut Continental Infantry and was then commissioned November 24, 1785, in the federal army. Married Mary Boardman January 16, 1790,

The Eastern Gateway Visitor's Center, as seen through the northern gate of Fort Steuben.

Middletown. Little Turtle attacked a detachment of Harmar's men under Colonel John Hardin on October 20; they were utterly defeated. Harmar sent a second detachment after Little Turtle; it was this detachment that included Frothingham, and he was killed.

CAPTAIN JOHN FRANCIS HAMTRAMCK (1756–April 11, 1803)—French Canadian recruited out of New York for the Continental army 1775; commissioned captain U.S. infantry April 12, 1785; commanding officer in charge of his own and two other companies building Fort Steuben; received field promotion while at the fort in April 1786, though it was not officially recorded until October 20.

CAPTAIN JONATHAN HEART (1748–1791)—Yale class of 1768; promoted captain June 9, 1785; arrived at Fort Steuben September 1, 1786; mentioned by Hamtramck as being on the line January 2, 1787. After serving in Fort Steuben, he joined St. Clair's Second Infantry and was killed in an Indian attack near Fort Recovery, Ohio, November 4, 1791.

ANDREW HENDERSON—one of the deputy geographers assigned to the Seven Ranges of the Northwest Ordinance; signed Hutchins's proclamation dated September 1, 1786; sent by Pennsylvania, Henderson was one of two surveyors with military training as an officer. He served with the Third Pennsylvania Regiment in the Revolution, commissioned as ensign December 31, 1779, promoted lieutenant August 12, 1784, resigned two months later.

ADAM HOOPS (January 9, 1760–June 9, 1846)—Pennsylvania surveyor to whom John Matthews reported August 16, 1786. Mentioned in Beatty's diary, September 22, 1786. Commander of Fort Jay, New York, from 1798 to 1800.

HOPOCAN (1740?–1818?)—trading name of Konieschquanoheel, the chief of the Wolf Clan of the Delaware from 1773 to 1818. The name means "tobacco pipe," so he was known in English documents as "Captain Pipe." The Fort Steuben surveyors looked to him for safe passage in the Ohio Valley—until September 13, 1786, when he told Hutchins he could no longer guarantee the safety of the surveyors.

CAPTAIN THOMAS HUTCHINS (1730–1789)—born Monmouth County, New Jersey; appointed geographer of the United States, 1781; surveyors reported to him. His rank was honorary.

LIEUTENANT WILLIAM KERSEY (d. 21 March 1800)—born in New Jersey, where he was recruited by the First New Jersey Regiment; commissioned First American Regiment November 24, 1785. Given temporary command of Mercer's regiment in October 1786, apparently due to Mercer's disobedience in distributing the wool overalls; Hamtramck praised Kersey's industriousness in building the fort. On August 31, 1786, Kersey led a detachment from Mercer's company to root out squatters.

ISRAEL LUDLOW (1765–January 20, 1804)—ran the seventh range. His later activities in settling the lower Ohio Valley are better known; he founded his own town, Ludlow's Station, in 1790 and laid the boundaries for Dayton.

ENSIGN FRANCIS LUSE—born in New Jersey, volunteered as a private with the Second Regiment New Jersey Continental Infantry in 1777; commissioned ensign in Lieutenant Colonel William DeHart's company, June 17, 1780; served at siege of Yorktown. Served as quartermaster at Fort Steuben. Lost his commission in 1790 after being dismissed for drunkenness on duty.

ABSALOM MARTIN (1758–1801)—one of the eight state geographers assigned to survey the Seven Ranges of the Northwest Ordinance; Martin represented New Jersey. Martin made the first range line after the geographer's line had been laid, August 11, 1786, and surveyed the second range the following month. After the establishment of St. Clair as territorial governor, Martin was the first to be granted a license (December 28, 1789) to ferry the Ohio River, hence the name of Martins Ferry, Ohio.

A Fort Steuben Who's Who, 1786–1787

JOHN MATTHEWS (February 18, 1765–October 31, 1828)—quartermaster at Fort Steuben after February 8, 1787; nephew of General Rufus Putnam, the "Father of Ohio"; Matthews's diary of the Fort Steuben days is a valuable resource.

CAPTAIN WILLIAM McCURDY (d. 1822)—led one of the companies that built Fort Steuben. Born in Pennsylvania, where he was recruited for the Continental infantry (First Pennsylvania, May 8, 1781). Promoted captain August 12, 1784 (four months junior to Hamtramck). Arrived at the camp that would be Fort Steuben September 29, 1786, almost two months after the other military captains. He was imprisoned briefly for insubordination but released after signing a writ claiming the breach was unintentional. He resigned his commission June 4, 1791, and died in 1822.

WILLIAM McMAHON—lawyer and Ohio County, Virginia magistrate whose homestead across the river from Mingo was frequented by Fort Steuben personnel; it was in his home that the surveyors did their "platting," or mapping of the townships in the Seven Ranges from mid-November 1786 to spring of 1787.

CAPTAIN JOHN MERCER—led one of the companies that completed the first blockhouse. Born in and recruited from New Jersey; promoted captain November 24, 1785. Mercer had been taken prisoner by the British February 1, 1777, and exchanged November 6, 1780. Resigned commission November 26, 1790.

CAPTAIN JOHN MILLS (d. 1796)—commissary of Fort Steuben according to Beatty's diary for September 22, 1786. At this time, the only fortifications would have been "redoubts." Served in the First Massachusetts Regiment in the Revolution, 1776; promoted captain May 3, 1779. Commanded Fifth Company at West Point, 1784.

SAMUEL MONTGOMERY (1740–1808)—one of the deputy geographers assigned to survey the Seven Ranges of the Northwest Ordinance.

WILLIAM W. MORRIS (1757–1832)—one of the eight state geographers assigned to survey the Seven Ranges of the Northwest Ordinance, Morris arrived at Hamtramck's camp September 1, 1786.

MAJOR WILLIAM NORTH (1755–January 3, 1836)—Baron von Steuben's aide-de-camp in the Revolution; mustered the three companies of surveyors who built Fort Steuben and later told the baron about the fort named after him.

LIEUTENANT WILLIAM PETERS—commissary until replaced by Matthews February 8, 1787; born in New York, where he enlisted in the Second New York Continental Infantry during the Revolution. His commission is dated June 27, 1786, which means that Fort Steuben was his very first assignment in the

A view of the guardhouse from outside Fort Steuben, facing west.

federal army. In September 1786, while assisting Colonel Sproat in surveying, his horse disappeared; after following the horse's tracks for several miles, Peters concluded that the horses were stolen by Indians (Hutchins, October 12, 1786).

POMOACAN, "HALF-KING" (d. 1788)—leader of the Wyandot at the time of the treaties; met with Jacob Springer at Sandusky September 1, 1786, during the surveying of the Seven Ranges.

MAJOR WINTHROP SARGENT (May 1, 1753–June 3, 1820)—surveyor representing New Hampshire, though he was from Massachusetts; he became a secretary of the Ohio Company in 1787. Sargent, a member of the American Academy of Arts & Sciences, as well as the Philosophical Society, surveyed the fifth range. Married Rowena Tupper (1767–1790), daughter of fellow surveyor Benjamin Tupper, February 6, 1789—first marriage in the territory (Marietta). Rowena died in childbirth January 29, 1790.

ENSIGN CORNELIUS RYKER SEYDAM—mentioned in Hamtramck's letter of May 10, 1787, as leading a detachment against the squatters, destroying twelve houses. Recruited from New Jersey as ensign, March 17, 1786; served in the First New Jersey Regiment in the Revolution.

A FORT STEUBEN WHO'S WHO, 1786–1787

COLONEL ISAAC SHERMAN—a surveyor sent by Connecticut, though apparently not one of the eight "state geographers"; helped establish Connecticut's claim to the "Western Reserve." Hutchins refers to him as "Colonel."

JAMES SIMPSON—one of the eight state geographers assigned to survey the Seven Ranges of the Northwest Ordinance; Simpson was sent by the state of Maryland. Finney calls him "Captain" (August 29, 1786).

CHARLES SMITH—one of the eight state geographers assigned to survey the Seven Ranges of the Northwest Ordinance.

CAPTAIN JOHN SMITH (d. June 6, 1811)—recruited from Massachusetts; led one of the companies in the evacuation of Fort Steuben May 30, 1787.

CAPTAIN JACOB SPRINGER—Indian scout for the geographic team, brought Hutchins word in September 1786 of agitation against the surveyors.

COLONEL EBENEZER SPROAT (1752–1805)—official surveyor for Rhode Island, surveyed the fourth range; later a major stockholder of the Ohio Company. Very tall; known to the Indians as "Hetuch" (Eye of Buck), became known as "Big Buckeye." He was six feet, four inches tall; this is one explanation for

The inside of the upper floor of the blockhouse, looking at the gun ports. This floor would only be used in case of attack.

the source of the nickname for Ohio. Appointed brigade inspector by Baron von Steuben in the Revolution.

CAPTAIN DAVID STRONG (d. August 19, 1801)—led a company from Fort Steuben to Fort Harmar; promoted captain July 15, 1785; born in Connecticut.

CAPTAIN ANDREW VAN SWEARINGEN (1742–December 2, 1793)—mentioned in McMahon's September 21, 1786 letter to Hutchins as the builder of "Cox's Fort," a single blockhouse in what is now Wellsburg, West Virginia. Van Swearingen settled near the northeast boundary of Wellsburg about the same time as the Cox brothers (September 1772). Hutchins employed him as a hunter on the surveying party; on September 25, 1786, he sighted an Indian near the surveyors' camp.

ANSELM TUPPER (October 11, 1763–December 25, 1808)—son of Massachusetts geographer Benjamin Tupper; worked with his father on the fifth range.

BENJAMIN TUPPER (March 11, 1738–June 16, 1792)—one of the eight state geographers assigned to survey the Seven Ranges for the Northwest Ordinance. One of several surveyors with military experience, Tupper had been a general before the close of the Revolution. Tupper, with his friend Rufus Putnam, placed the ad in the Massachusetts newspapers that led to the formation of the Ohio Company, which lobbied Congress to survey the west.

TURIS—Lenape messenger sent by Hutchins August 4, 1786, to ask for protection from the Lenape against other Indian nations.

BIBLIOGRAPHY

Anonymous. *Historical Account of Bouquet's Expedition Against the Ohio Indians, 1764*. Philadelphia, PA, 1765.

Beatty, Charles C. "Origin of Fort Steuben." *Daily Herald* [Steubenville], September 14, 1850, 2.

Beatty, Ekuries. "Diary." *Magazine of American History* 1 (1877), 175–438.

Bond, Beverly W., Jr. *The Foundations of Ohio*. Vol. I of Carl Wittke, *The History of the State of Ohio*. Columbus: Ohio State Archaeological and Historical Society, 1941.

Butler, James R. "Journal of General Butler." *Olden Time* 2, no. 10 (October 1847): 433–531.

Caldwell, J.A. *History of Belmont and Jefferson Counties, Ohio*. Wheeling, WV: Historical Publication Company, 1880.

Davies, Charles. *The Elements of Surveying*. New York: J&J Harper, 1830.

Doyle, Joseph B. *Twentieth Century History of Steubenville and Jefferson County, Ohio*. Chicago: Richmond-Arnold Publishing Co., 1910.

Ernst, Joseph W. *With Compass and Chain: Federal Land Surveyors in the Old Northwest, 1785–1816*. New York: Arno Press, 1979. Reprint of a Columbia University MA thesis, 1958.

Harmar, Josiah. The Harmar Papers. Early Americana Collection, William L. Clemens Library, University of Michigan, Ann Arbor. Letters in this collection are identified in the text by date.

Heart, Jonathan. *Journal of Captain Jonathan Heart*. Albany, NY: Joel Munsell's Sons, 1885.

Heitman, Francis B. *Historical Register and Dictionary of the United States Army, From Its Organization, September 29, 1789, to March 2, 1903*. Washington, D.C.: Government Printing Office, 1903.

Hicks, F.C. "Thomas Hutchins." *Dictionary of American Biography*, vol. 5. New York: Scribners, 1961, 435–36.

Hulbert, Archer Butler. "The Indian Thoroughfares of Ohio." *Ohio Archaeological and Historical Publications* 8 (1900): 264–95.

Hurt, R. Douglas. *The Ohio Frontier*. Bloomington: Indiana University Press, 1996.

Hutchins, Thomas. *The Courses of the Ohio River (1766)*. Edited by Beverly W. Bond, Jr. Cincinnati: Historical and Philosophical Society of Ohio, 1942.

King, Elizabeth. *Fort Steuben: 1786–1790. The Seven Ranges and the Northwest Territory*. Steubenville, OH: Old Fort Steuben Project, Inc., 1987.

Knepper, George W. *Ohio and Its People*. Kent, OH: Kent State University Press, 2003.

Linklater, Andro. *Measuring America: How the United States Was Shaped by the Greatest Land Sale in History*. New York: Plume Books, 2003.

Powell, Colonel William H. *List of Officers of the Army of the United States from 1779 to 1900*. New York: L.R. Hamersly & Co., 1900.

Roberts, Robert B. *Encyclopedia of Historic Forts*. New York: Macmillan, 1988.

Sherman, C.E. *Original Ohio Land Subdivisions, Being Volume III Final Report*. N.p.: Ohio State Reformatory, 1925.

Smith, William Henry. *The St. Clair Papers: The Life and Public Services of Arthur St. Clair*. Cincinnati, OH: Robert Clarke & Co., 1882.

Steuben, Frederick William Baron von. *Regulations for the Order and Discipline of the Troops of the United States*. Boston: Thomas and Andrews, 1794.

White, C. Albert. *A History of the Rectangular Survey System*. Washington, D.C.: U.S. Department of the Interior, Bureau of Land Management, 1983.

ABOUT THE AUTHOR

John R. Holmes grew up in western New York and studied at St. Bonaventure and Kent State Universities. Since 1985, he has taught English at Franciscan University of Steubenville. His fascination with Steubenville's history began in 1991 when he was asked to portray the city's namesake, Baron Friedrich Wilhelm von Steuben (1730–1794). Dr. Holmes lives in Steubenville with his wife, Von, and sons Greg, Scott and Luke, and their Grandma McGeehan. Holmes's first book for The History Press, *Remembering Steubenville: From Frontier Fort to Steel Valley*, was published in 2009.

Visit us at
www.historypress.net

·